SYMPTOMS, ILLNESS BEHAVIOR, AND HELP-SEEKING

Monographs in Psychosocial Epidemiology

SYMPTOMS, ILLNESS BEHAVIOR, AND HELP-SEEKING

edited by David Mechanic

Publication of this book has been assisted by a grant from the Commonwealth Fund. The Fund is not responsible for viewpoints and conclusions of the authors.

PRODIST
New York-1982

First published in the United States by
PRODIST
a division of
Neale Watson Academic Publications, Inc.
156 Fifth Avenue, New York, NY 10010

Library of Congress Cataloging in Publication Data
Main entry under title:

Symptoms, illness behavior, and help-seeking.

(Monographs in psychosocial epidemiology; v. 3)
Includes bibliographies.
Contents: The epidemiology of illness behavior and its relationship to physical and psychological distress/David Mechanic—Uses and abuses of the Langner index/R. Blair Wheaton—Self-regulation and the mechanisms for symptom appraisal/Howard Leventhal, David R. Nerenz, Andrea Straus—[etc.]
1. Health behavior—United States. 2. Help-seeking behavior—United States. 3. Symptomatology. 4. Epidemiology—United States. I. Mechanic, David, 1936- . II. Series. [DNLM: 1. Sick role. 2. Patient acceptance of health care. WM 178 S989]
RA776.9.S95 1982 362.1'042 82-3856
ISBN 0-88202-134-6 (pbk.) AACR2

Designed and manufactured in the U.S.A.

Table of Contents

Foreword: A Series in Psychosocial Epidemiology — vii
B. Z. Locke
A. E. Slaby

Preface — 11
B. Z. Locke
A. E. Slaby

The Epidemiology of Illness Behavior and Its Relationship to Physical and Psychological Distress — 1
David Mechanic

Uses and Abuses of the Langner Index: A Reexamination of Findings on Psychological and Psychophysiological Distress — 25
Blair Wheaton

Self-Regulation and the Mechanisms for Symptom Appraisal — 55
Howard Leventhal
David R. Nerenz
Andrea Straus

No Time for Depression: A Study of Help-Seeking Among Mothers of Preschool Children — 87
Susannah Ginsberg
George W. Brown

Psychosocial Disorders in Primary Medical Care — 115
Paul Williams
Michael Shepherd

Help-Seeking in Severe Mental Illness — 135
John A. Clausen
Nancy G. Pfeffer
Carol L. Huffine

Notes on Contributors — 156

Foreword

Rising costs of mental health care and interest in the development of a national health insurance that should include some mental health services have heightened concern for ways by which health planners may evaluate the extent of behavioral problems and the means by which the efficacy of various treatment modalities may be assessed. Questions of paramount importance include: If there exist two or more ways of treating an illness, which is the most effective? If two therapeutic modalities are equally effective, which is the most efficient? If equally efficient, which is the least costly? Questions regarding the prevalence and incidence rates of specific psychiatric illness in communities are being raised by those delegated with the task of making policy recommendations for programs of primary prevention and treatment. What is the natural history of a behavioral problem untreated and how is the problem affected by normal growth and development? What does a knowledge of the natural history of a disorder of mood, thought, or behavior tell us about its etiology, and how may it lead to methods of prevention? If an illness is not preventable by currently available knowledge, what interventions may be made in its natural history to arrest and possibly reverse its course? Mental health is now big business, and failure to look at specific population needs when planning programs and to build in ways of evaluating cost-efficiency-effectiveness results in considerable psychological and economic cost to millions of patients and their families as well as taxpayers in general.

Epidemiology includes a number of technical skills used in answering some of the questions facing health planners today. Traditionally, epidemiology has been seen as the study of disease patterns in populations. Epidemiologists have been useful in providing data that have led to effective programs of prevention of a number of infectious diseases including malaria, smallpox, and poliomyelitis. However, epidemiology has played a minor role in psychiatric research until relatively recently. Epidemiologic studies in mental health tended to be descriptive and focused on the prevalence and incidence rates of symptoms in broad diagnostic categories of illness such as "neuroses" or "psychoses." In fact, some infectious- and chronic-disease epidemiologists question whether epidemiology can be used to tackle psychiatric problems. The Society for Epidemiologic Research does not have a section on psychosocial epidemiology, and the publication of papers in social and psychiatric epidemiology in the main journal of epidemiology is infrequent. The principal organs of dispersion of knowledge in psychosocial epidemiology have been *Psychological Medicine* and the *Archives of General Psychiatry.* The former journal, published quarterly, has on its editorial board members that are sophisticated in epidemiology and probably publishes the greatest number of articles in this area. As a British journal it has limited readership in the United States. The *Archives of General Psychiatry*, a publication of the American Medical Association, is widely read in the United States. It publishes a number of high-quality papers in epidemiology but has a broad mandate and, therefore, is limited in its ability to publish more.

The *Monograph Series in Psychosocial Epidemiology*, of which this is the third volume, is to serve several important functions for epidemiology, psychiatry, and related areas in public health. The objectives include:

1. Providing a forum for discussion of research strategies in the evaluation of mental health problems in the community and of assessing effectiveness of psychiatric treatment interventions;
2. Serving as a teaching tool for students in medical schools and schools of public health, hospital administration, social work, and nursing, as well as for students in departments of psychology and sociology and, especially, epidemiology;
3. Keeping prospective researchers alert to problems needing investigation in the area of psychosocial epidemiology;
4. Serving as a vehicle to bring together research in the area of psychosocial epidemiology;
5. Providing a means of continuing education for epidemiologists working in the field; and
6. Providing a means for discussions on how the results of epidemiologic and related behavioral research might be brought to bear on the development of state and federal health policy decisions.

To achieve these ends, each monograph will have a theme of particular interest to investigators in the field of psychosocial epidemiology such as the study of children, the study of stressful life events, and needs assessment. Each volume of the monograph will have a guest editor with an established reputation in the field chosen by us. The guest editor will direct the selection of the individual contributors and write the introductory article. In general, the lead article will: (1) contain a discussion of methodological considerations in research of a given area (i.e., experimental design, sampling, instruments used, analysis of data, economic considerations and ethical decisions in planning studies), (2) critically review existing studies, (3) present information on the current state of the field, and (4) suggest directions for further research.

The volumes in the series to follow this one on the study of symptoms, illness behavior, and help-seeking, include ones on needs assessment, genetics, aging, alcohol use, ethics of epidemiologic research, drug use, community surveys, and the methodology of natural experiments. Earlier volumes have dealt with studies of children and the evaluation of stressful life events and their contexts. Guest editors include Barbara Snell Dohrenwend and Bruce P. Dohrenwend, Felton Earls, Carl Eisdorfer, Stanislav V. Kasl, Jerome Myers, Lee N. Robins, Marc Schuckett, Laurence R. Tancredi, Ming T. Tsuang, George Warheit, and Myrna M. Weissman. In addition to the introductory article and papers by selected investigators in the field, each issues will contain, whenever possible, an editorial appearing as the Afterword written by a representative of the World Health Organization and a Preface written by ourselves. The representative of WHO, chosen by Dr. Norman Sartorius, Director of the Division of Mental Health, will focus on what is being done internationally in the topic area; what WHO feels are research priorities in the field; and what particular methodological problems in research in the area exist in pretechnological and Third World nations. Our editorial will address the present state of epidemiologic research in the area, the directions the Center for Epidemiologic Studies at the National Institute of Mental Health would like to see research take, and the relationship of research in the field to the formulation of health policy.

The mandate of this series is challenging and the task great, but with the help of our guest editors and other contributors, and feedback from our readership, we can make the series special and sufficient to fulfill the need for an organ to draw together researchers, students, and health-policy makers in an effort to reap from research in psychosocial epidemiology conclusions that lead to effective and consumer-responsive health policy and programs of preventive psychiatric care.

B.Z.L.
A.E.S.

Preface

Psychological or medical symptoms may be a *necessary* cause in most cases but taken alone are not a *sufficient* cause for the use of health care services. Studies in both the United States and Great Britian (White et al., 1961) have demonstrated that in an average month, for every 1,000 individuals aged 16 or older, about 750 will experience what they indentify as an episode of illness or injury characterized by a need for some definitive action such as the use of medication, bed rest, or limitation of activity. Only about one-third of these, however, consult a physician for help. Comparably, large-scale epidemiologic studies using a number of measures with various cutoff points have shown that as many as 60 to 80 percent of individuals have psychological symptoms at any given time (Dohrenwend and Dohrenwend, 1969; Leighton, 1957; Srole et al., 1962), and that about one-fourth to one-third of these are seriously impaired by their symptoms. While psychiatrists in their writing and therapeutic practice have often viewed psychological symptoms as a sufficient and necessary condition for seeking help, many symptomatic people neither see themselves as being in need of psychiatric care nor as having a problem (Linn, 1962). In the Midtown Manhattan Study (Srole et al., 1962) for instance, less than a quarter of those with psychiatric problems ever sought help. Factors that have been identified as influencing the decision to seek help when an individual becomes symptomatic include sex, socioeconomic status, religion, ethnic and social background, age, friend's attitude toward help-seeking, life events, perception of the meaning of bodily change, personality factors, and social supports.

The increased awareness of the fact that both the quantity and the severity of medical and psychological symptoms explain only a small part of the variance of help-seeking from formal health caregivers has important implications for health policy makers. Community surveys of symptoms or "illness" behavior without regard to the plethora of psychosocial and economic variables that work together to determine whether a symptomatic or "sick" person will seek help can lead to the malappropriation of millions of health-care dollars for community-based programs that will go unused. For example, it is well known that individuals over 65 years of age comprise approximately 10 percent of the United States population but consume as much as 30 percent of our health resources. Epidemiologic community surveys of this groups, however, found that while the elderly score significantly higher on manifest symptoms scales and measures of neuropsychiatric impairment they utilize only a small fraction of psychiatric services (Goldfarb, 1962; Slaby, 1978; Teeter et al., 1976). A health planner unsophisticated in what factors influence utilization of health-care services may ill-advisedly promote the construction of a large community mental health center or private psychiatric clinic in a sector of the city with a predominantly older population only to find that the modern diagnostic, assessment, and treatment services available go unused. Comparably, well-intentioned politicians may support the development of state or federally funded drug programs for adolescents following an epidemic of substance abuse in the inner city or suicide prevention centers after an outbreak of adolescent suicide attempts, only to find that these services are neglected in preference to the use of "grass roots" drug drop-in centers or crises centers with little external funding and staffed by youth volunteers in a church basement or old storefront.

Knowledge of the psychosocial determinants of help-seeking behavior also plays an important role in helping consumers obtain from health-care providers services that address their real (rather than perceived) needs. Meeting health-care consumers' *real* as opposed to their *overt* reasons for seeking medical care would be posited to reduce health-care cost and the need for unneccessary clinical and laboratory diagnostic tests and hospitalizations, and studies have indicated that it does. It is apparent from research already performed that individuals may obtain succor and support at a time of intrapsychic conflict resulting from such stresses as marital distress, termination of a love affair, and difficulty at work or school by seeking help for medical symptoms that are no more intense or frequent than (*a*) those of other individuals around them who do not seek help or, (*b*) are different in intensity or frequency from symptoms they themselves had before, when their life was happier and less disrupted and they did not seek help. In a study of a prepaid health maintenance organization, it was found that utilization of medical and auxiliary laboratory services declined significantly in high utilizers who received a course of psychotherapy, while that of matched controls not receiving therapy did not. Brief therapy and one session groups had the largest decline in utilization of services thought to be sought for purely "medical reasons," thereby offsetting the cost of treatment. Clearly, health-care costs can be reduced and health expenditures more "cost-contained" if health policy makers provide services for health-care consumers that are consistent with what we know about what *really* makes people seek medical health rather than what *appears* to make them seek help.

Although the National Institute of Mental Health (NIMH) has had an interest in and has provided grant support for health-services research, it lacked the specific, scientifically rigorous research herein recommended. In 1980 the Division of Biometry and Epidemiology of NIMH initiated a new grant program to support mental health service system research needed if health policy makers are to improve their decision-making ability.

The guest editor of volume 3 of our series *Monographs in Psychosocial Epidemiology*, David Mechanic, is prominent in the field of the understanding of the interrelations between psychosocial and economic variables and symptoms, illness behavior, and help-seeking. His paper, coupled with those of the contributing authors he has selected, addresses the occurrence of symptoms and illness in populations, how these symptoms and illness are perceived, the pathways to care, and the responses of health professionals. Measures of symptoms and illness in populations have improved significantly in the past two decades, resulting in increased attention being focused today on the complex processes affecting the conditions under which help is sought. In his overview chapter Dr. Mechanic outlines some of the major approaches used in studying illness behavior and help-seeking with consideration given to the benefits and disadvantages of large-scale multivariate surveys. Determinants of illness behavior are examined, focusing on research on the acquisition of health attitudes and behavior, vocabularies of distress, illness behavior as a mode of coping, and symptom definition. The interrelationships between physical and psychological symptoms are stressed throughout, and the difficulties of distinguishing illness from illness behavior are emphasized. Some provocative lines of research inquiry are suggested.

The Langner 22-item scale is one of the most frequently used indications of psychological and/or psychophysiological distress. Blair Wheaton explores the relationship of this scale, and subparts of it, to both physical and psychiatric disorders. While in recent years this scale has received much criticism as a measure of psychiatric symptomatology, it is robust and is positively correlated with costly and apparently more sophisticated screening measures. Most of these measures appear to tap a general state of distress that Dohrenwend calls demoralization, thus explaining the difficulty of achieving useful differentiation. Wheaton brings new evidence to bear on the usefulness of the Langner Index and suggests that criticisms may be exaggerated.

Biases in symptom reporting and use of medical services are considered from a psychological perspective in the next chapter.

Based on a processing model of how people deal with illness threats, Leventhal and his coauthors describe how biases in epidemiologic statistics can be produced at all stages of an illness episode. Following a brief presentation of the model, the authors discuss its implications for understanding the stages of symptom generation, interpretation, care-seeking, and assessment of treatment effectiveness. Emphasis is placed on people's need to relate abstract information about illness to their own concrete experience of symptoms. The authors include in their discussion recommendations for research and public policy.

The final three contributions to this volume represent recent developments in help-seeking research. Ginsberg and Brown describe vividly a study documenting the failure of primary care providers and family members to recognize and appropriately manage clinical depression in a group of women in north London. Their work illustrates how tentative and uncertain help-seeking and the help-giving process can be. Williams and Shepherd, recognizing the uncertainty of adequate recognition and care, present results of an innovative demonstration on how such care can be provided more adequately. In the final chapter, Clausen, Pfeffer, and Huffine present the first detached description of help-seeking processes among the severely mentally ill over an extended period of time, thereby giving us some understanding of a neglected area, and suggesting many new questions for continuing inquiry.

Readers of this volume should gain a heightened sensitivity to the complex relationship between symptoms, illness behavior, and help-seeking and a clearer understanding of what factors must be taken into consideration when designing studies of how to best construct health-care services that are both cost-effective-efficient and consumer responsive and responsible.

References

Dohrenwend, B.P. and Dohrenwend, B.S. (1969), *Social Status and Psychological Disorder*. New York, Wiley-Interscience.

Goldfarb, A.I. (1962), Prevalence of psychiatric disorders in metropolitan old age and nursing homes. *J. Am. Geriat. Soc.* 10:77–84.

Leighton, D. (1956), Community study of mental health: Preliminary findings on the distribution of persons with symptoms of psychiatric significance in relation to social environment. In *The Nature and Transmission of the Genetic and Cultural Characteristics of Human Populations*. New York, Milbank Memorial Fund, 68–77.

Linn, L.S. (1962), Social characteristics and social interaction in the utilization of a psychiatric outpatient clinic. *J. Hlth. Soc. Behav.*, 8:3–14.

Slaby, A.E. (1978), The Interface of Mental Health and Medicine in the Care of

Older Patients: What We Know. Gerontological Society Meetings, Dallas, Texas, November 16–17.

Srole, L., Langner, T.S., Michael, S.T., Opler, M.K., & Rennie, T.A.C. (1962), *Mental Health in the Metropolis; The Midtown Manhattan Study*, (Thomas A.C. Rennie Series in Social Psychiatry, Vol. 1). New York, McGraw-Hill.

Teeter, R.B., Geretz, F.K., Miller, W.R., & Heiland, W.F. (1976). Psychiatric disturbances of aged patients in skilled nursing homes. *Am. J. Psychiat.*, 133:1430–1434.

White, K.L., Williams, T.F., & Greenberg, B.G. (1961), The ecology of medical care. *New Eng. J. Med.*, 265:885–892.

The Epidemiology of Illness Behavior and Its Relationship to Physical and Psychological Distress

DAVID MECHANIC

Illness usually refers to a limited scientific concept denoting a constellation of symptoms or a condition underlying them (Mechanic, 1978a). Illness behavior, on the other hand, describes the manner in which persons monitor their bodies, define and interpret their symptoms, take remedial actions, and utilize the health-care system. People differentially perceive, evaluate, and respond to illness, and such behaviors have enormous influence on the extent to which illness interferes with usual life routines, the chronicity of the condition, the attainment of appropriate care, and the cooperation of the patient in the treatment situation.

Physicians and patients tend to view health status in fundamentally different ways. Physicians are trained to identify specific illnesses and have no adequate measures of holistic functioning, vitality, or well-being. Although patients may become concerned about specific symptoms, they conceive of health status in terms of an overall sense of well-being and the extent to which the symptoms they experience disrupt their ability to function or interfere in some significant fashion with their life activities. A variety of studies indicate that people's emotional states influence their sense of physical well-being (Apple, 1960; Baumann, 1961). Persons reporting poor physical health are frequently depressed, feel neglected, have low morale, suffer from alienation, and are less satisfied with life (Maddox, 1962). The causal sequence obviously can go both ways.

Tessler and Mechanic (1978), using multivariate controls, analyzed four diverse data sets to examine the relationship between psychological distress and perceptions of physical health. In each case, distress was a significant factor related to the perceptions of physical health. A recent review of the literature by investigators at Rand also supports the observation that general health measures have an important psychological component (Ware et al., 1978).

Moreover, in a prospective study of utilization among enrollees of a prepaid group practice, Tessler, Mechanic, and Dimond (1976) found that the level of psychological distress was a significant factor predicting utilization levels of general medical services while controlling for a wide range of other variables including health status measures. In short, psychological orientations affect not only people's views of their health but also their patterns of health care utilization.

Modes of Studying Illness Behavior: Methodological Considerations

Although there is a large medical literature on the patient's hidden agenda in seeking medical care and on a variety of related issues, medical researchers have had difficulty in posing the relevant issues in a manner amenable to empirical research. There are at least four ways in which illness behavior can be studied: as a disposition of the person, as a result of an interaction between personal and environmental factors in a community, as a response to the health care services system, or as a decision-making process.

The Dispositional Approach—The dispositional approach assumes that persons have a fairly stable pattern of response to illness and seeks to identify differences in these patterns and in ways they develop. While some persons tend to respond stoically in the face of illness, others are matter-of-fact or hypochondriacal. While some patients seek care readily for even minor symptoms, others are reluctant to seek care even for life-threatening illnesses. The point to remember is that the disposition is a research assumption and not necessarily a reality. There is considerable variability in people's responses from one situation to another and over time, and we have insufficient data on the stability of health and illness behavior patterns over time to feel fully confident in the dispositional assumption. Thus it is simply a convenience for the purposes of acquiring more knowledge.

Reactions to pain or dispositions to use various kinds of medical services may be measured by verbal reports of what respondents would do in hypothetical situations or by their actual behavior such as consulting a psychiatrist, joining a self-help group, or practicing transcendental meditation. The fact of having used one of these services serves as a proxy for the disposition, and the investigator then tries to identify the factors associated with the response of interest. Unfortunately most such dispositional studies have not been theoretically oriented and, thus, have not gone beyond description of basic sociodemographic factors. As a result, they contribute only in a limited way to understanding the dynamic processes of illness response.

Most dispositional studies are efforts to understand the development of the behavior pattern. For example, many studies of illness show that women report symptoms more frequently than men do and also that they use physicians and psychiatrists more frequently (Lewis and Lewis, 1977; Mechanic, 1976c). A variety of interpretations have been posited to account for these findings, but none adequately explains all of the available data. Interpretations for the sex differences include the hypothesis that there are real differences in the prevalence of disorder. Some other explanations are that characteristics of the measures used and judgments made reflect sex biases, women's lower thresholds to perceive symptoms, women's greater willingness to acknowledge symptoms and seek care, women's greater knowledge and interest in health matters, and different role responsibilities between the sexes that affect the use of services. Differences in prevalence of symptoms may be explained by differential stress among men and women, by different vulnerabilities to stressors, varying levels of coping resources and skills, and different networks of social support. Although each of these interpretations is given from time to time, few studies successfully compare competing explanations (Mechanic, 1976c).

Significant differences in responses to pain and illness between the sexes are already apparent by the fourth grade and increase with age (Mechanic, 1964). Aggregate data on sex and use of medical care suggest that women have higher rates of utilization at all ages, except during childhood when the mother probably makes most of the decisions for both boys and girls. Lewis and his colleagues (1975), however, have shown that sex differences in using a school health service were apparent among young children in an experimental child-initiated help-seeking system. How these differences arise, how they are sustained, and how they might be modified are important research issues.

The Broad Epidemiologic Survey—The most typical approach to studying illness behavior is to execute epidemiologic surveys and identify those using or not using certain types of care or those who engage in particular health and illness practices. Other data from the surveys are then used to account for these differences. Such surveys typically examine sociodemographic factors, distress, life-change events, and attitudes toward medical care. Among factors commonly found to be associated with utilization of medical care are quality and severity of physical symptoms, levels of distress, sex, inclination to use medical facilities, skepticism of medical care, and faith in doctors.

A major problem with most epidemiologic studies of help-seeking is that they fail to differentiate the extent to which various independent predictors affect utilization through their influence on the occurrence of symptoms and the extent to which they have an independent effect on the help-seeking pattern (Mechanic, 1976b). Moreover, in concentrating on studying only one source of assistance, such as general physician services or a psychiatric clinic, these studies cannot differentiate factors that predict help-seeking in general as compared with those that predict the use of a specific type of service. Studies of use of multiple agencies by a specified population are extremely difficult to execute because of the complexity of the American health-care system and modes of payment. These studies usually require an enrolled population using a defined set of helping agencies.

Gurin and associates (1960), in a national survey of definitions and reactions to personal problems, suggested that different types of factors influence various aspects of the help-seeking process, such as identification of the problem, the decision to seek care, and the type of practitioner consulted. Greenley and Mechanic (1976) studied the patterns of use of helping facilities for psychological distress syndromes among a large student population. Among the types of sources of help studied were psychiatrists, counseling services, religious counselors, general physicians, and other agencies on campus. There was considerable overlap in the problems brought to different sources of help, and most predictors of help-seeking were specific to particular sources of assistance.

It was difficult to identify factors predicting help-seeking in general compared to those specifically predicting going to a psychiatrist, a clergyman, or a general physician. Among students with a tendency to seek help for psychological problems as measured by hypothetical items, women and those with introspective orientations were more inclined to use most types of helping services including psychiatrists, counseling, and general physicians. In contrast, most other predictors were linked specifically to certain types of providers. A disproportionate number of women, Jewish students, students with no religious affiliation, those from the eastern United States, and those from more educated and affluent families were more likely to use psychiatric services. Students who scored high on countercultural orientations were much more likely to use psychiatry than other sources of assistance. Catholics and students with more religious participation went to religious counselors. Younger students, unmarried students, and those with less distinctive social and cultural orientations were more likely to use student counseling than student psychiatry. However, the characteristics of students using any of a variety of sources of help were not very different than the characteristics of the population as a whole. Sociocultural characteristics, attitudes, knowledge, reference group orientations, and degree of psychological distress all had independent effects on the use of helping services. In sum, it appears that symptoms and distress are triggers that initiate the patient's search and evaluation process. Social and cultural attitudes and orientations tend to shape this evaluative process and the decisions made about appropriate ways of coping. This can be investigated through studies of symptom attribution.

Symptom Attribution—A third approach to studying illness behavior, thus, is to focus on the processes through which persons identify and evaluate symptoms, make interpretations of their causes and implications, and decide on the types of help to seek. Persons experiencing changes in their emotional states and physical functioning attempt to make sense of what is happening, and they tend to examine different intuitive hypotheses about the seriousness of their problems and the need for assistance. A major dimension of this process is the way people evaluate the causes of a problem and the extent to which they attribute the problem to external factors, internal difficulties, or moral and existential issues. An important function of health education is to shape such processes of evaluation and attribution so that they culminate in an effective pattern of care. Understanding attribution processes and the ways to modify them has many rehabilitative implications (Mechanic, 1977).

For example, during World War II soldiers who experienced "breakdowns" in combat were evacuated to the back lines, and their disorganized behavior was interpreted as a product of early childhood socialization. This provided the soldier with an excuse for maintaining his behavior and one that made it difficult to return him to a functioning role. The military later developed a policy that defined combat stress reactions as transient responses. Although soldiers were given opportunites to rest, the behavior was defined as a normal reaction to prolonged stress, and most soldiers were expected to return to active duty. As a result, there were many less psychiatric losses (Glass, 1958). These policies are now used in community care of the mentally ill, and it is clear that patients suffering from considerable distress and impairment can continue to cope in many realms of their lives. Although such "normalization" can be carried too far, the evidence is that the encouragement of continued coping and activity often protects the patient from further deterioration and despair, and that patients are very much influenced by social expectations (Brown et al., 1966).

The interpretation of symptoms may have a dramatic effect on the course of illness and disability. Many problems may be defined as inherent in a person or related to social, cultural, or environmental factors. An example is the growth of the women's movement, which has brought about a major shift in the way many women interpret the discomforts and dissatisfactions they feel. While prior to this movement many women who felt a sense of malaise thought of this as a unique personal problem, the emergence of women's groups has provided new interpretations. Instead of viewing their problems as a product of their inadequacies as women, wives, and mothers, women now receive support for explaining their distress as caused by existing inequalities, blocked opportunities, and exploitative role relationships. Women unhappy with their life circumstances are increasingly able to find others who support their explanations of distress as resulting from arrangements in the family and community rather than from their own inadequacies and failures. Similar groups are emerging among the disabled, the aged, and a variety of minorities. They contend that their problems are not simply a product of their status, but of social arrangements that exacerbate their limitations. In recent years research has repeatedly demonstrated that much of the disability associated with physical and mental illness is not an inherent product of the illness, but results from the manner in which the ill person responds to his or her condition and the manner in which it is managed. For example, much of the aggressive behavior previously associated with schizophrenia was a product of the violent way it was dealt with by the authorities rather than being an inherent feature of the syndrome (Eaton and Weil, 1955).

Influence of the Health-Care Services System—A fourth way of studying illness behavior is to examine the influence of varying features of the health-care system on the responses of the patient. One crucial determinant of help-seeking among patients is the accessibility of medical care (Lewis et al. 1976); and barriers to care may develop because of location, financial requirements, bureaucratic responses to the patient, social distance between client and professional, the lack of a regular or continuing relationship with an appropriate therapist, and stigma in seeking assistance. The point is that the problem often can be attacked more effectively by modifying the way agencies and professionals organize to deal with a problem than by attempting to change patient behavior. Organizational barriers affect patients differently (Mechanic, 1976a). Coinsurance and deductibles inhibit the poor more than the affluent; and aggressive, educated, and sophisticated patients can get what they want from medical bureaucracies more readily than can passive and less-informed patients. Similarly, such factors as distance to the site of care, waiting time, and a personal and continuing interest in the patient have different significance for varying population groups, and these must be understood for the effective organization of medical services.

The Effects of Methodology on Research Findings

While illness behavior and help-seeking are decisional processes that develop over time, most of our data come from large-scale, cross-sectional studies. Such studies have distinct advantages because they allow data collection from large numbers of people on a variety of indicators facilitating the use of sophisticated quantitative approaches. Taking a cross section of a complex psychosocial process has many costs, however, and often the measurements taken are only crude approximations of the process itself. Moreover, when all measurements of process are obtained at one point in time—and when the measures are general summaries of experience over time—the measures are often confounded and not amenable to clear causal analysis.

Some of these difficulties are illustrated by large-scale studies on physician utilization (Aday and Eichhorn, 1972; Andersen et al., 1975; Kohn and White, 1976; Wolinsky, 1978). There is an extensive literature on sociocultural and psychosocial factors affecting the definition of illness and decisions to use physicians (Kasl and Cobb, 1966a, 1966b; Robinson, 1971; Mechanic, 1978a), but in large-scale, cross-sectional studies these factors are found to be unimportant. Thus, while more intensive studies often note the significance of ethnicity, household structure, values and attitudes, learned inclinations, informal influences, and social distance to the extent that they are included in large-scale multivariate studies, they seem to be relatively insignificant as predictors.

A typical approach in the cross-sectional multivariate studies is to adopt a scheme developed by Andersen and his co-workers (1975) which conceives of physician utilization as a consequence of predisposing, enabling, and illness (need) variables. Predisposing variables refer to those that exist prior to the onset of illness and include demographic factors (age and sex, for example), social-structural variables (ethnicity, occupation, and education), and beliefs about medical care, physicians, and disease. Enabling factors "include family resources such as income and level of health insurance coverage or other source of third-party payment, and the existence, nature and accessibility of a regular source of health care" (p. 6). Community characteristics such as number of health facilities and personnel, region, or rural-urban nature of the community may also be relevant as enabling variables. Need may be divided into perceived need and evaluated need. For example, Andersen and his colleagues measured perceived need by (a) the number of reported bed days and other restricted activity days resulting from injury or illness, (b) number of symptoms reported from a checklist including such symptoms as "sudden feeling of weakness or faintness," "getting up some mornings tired and exhausted even with a usual amount of rest," "feeling tired for weeks at a time for no special reason," and "frequent headaches" (Aday and Andersen, 1975; Andersen et al., 1975), and (c) self-perceived general state of health. Evaluated illness includes symptom scores weighted by the extent to which physicians indicated that persons should see a doctor for these symptoms and physicians' ratings of the medical severity of the diagnoses reported in the interview.

Typically, such studies explain a modest amount of variance in physician contact (16 to 25 percent) using many predictors, and almost all of the variance explained is accounted for by "need" or "illness" variables. In Andersen's (1975) 1971 national study of health services utilization, for example, 85 percent of the variance in physician contact explained is accounted for by three perceived illness variables: worry about health (7.6 percent), disability days (4.8 percent), and symptoms (1.4 percent). In the case of volume of visits, diagnostic severity and perceived illness account for almost all of the 23.4 percent of variance explained: severity of diagnosis (14 percent), disability days (4.6 percent), symptoms (1.9 percent), perceived health (1 percent), worry about health (0.7 percent), and pain frequency (0.7 percent). Even less success in predicting utilization has been achieved in the International Collaborative Study (Kohn and White, 1976) (explaining 4 to 10 percent of the variance in adult utilization across geographic areas), and the variance explained was almost totally accounted for by "illness" variables.

The results of these multivariate studies can be attributed in part to gross measurement of subtle processes of response by summary measures that are not specific enough to capture important variations among respondents. Moreover, the variance attributed to "illness" in multivariate models that have only a very general theoretical rationale often masks the effects of important psychosocial processes. What are called "illness" and "need" in these studies are usually summary measures of illness behavior that incorporate psychological and attitudinal components and are correlated at a zero-order level with many relevant psychosocial measures. The introduction of the global illness measures in a regression equation simultaneous with other social and behavioral measures will often reduce the betas of such variables correlated with it to insignificance. From a theoretical standpoint, however, one should have a model that posits the interrelationships between the global illness behavior measures and other psychosocial factors.

The large-scale study of utilization is useful, however, because it allows the examination of many variables simultaneously and facilitates testing for spurious correlations. For such studies to be more valuable, however, specific theoretical models are required that hypothesize as clearly as possible the processes through which utilization is determined. Measurement must also be specific, must involve relatively short recall periods, and ideally should be sequential over some prospective time frame, capturing more closely important variations in illness response. Whenever possible, studies should be prospective, involving repeated measurement and/or linking data obtained during the interview with subsequent behavior as measured independently through observation, medical records, or other official documents. It is prudent to measure dependent variables independent of respondent reports if possible, because this limits distortions resulting from memory, the respondents' needs, or retrospective reconstruction.

Some Other Approaches to Physician Utilization—In addition to these multivariate approaches, other models have been suggested that focus to a larger degree on sociocultural and social-psychological issues. Antonovsky (1972), for example, suggests a model in which he includes host characteristics, characteristics of the medical institutions, and characteristics of the larger sociocultural environment. Host characteristics include latent need, intolerance of ambiguity of symptoms, and an orientation toward the use of professionals; medical system variables include availability of facilities, the ability to be responsive to various latent functions, and the degree of receptivity of physicians; and the sociocultural environment variables include organizational facilitation in using medical services, absence of stigma for such use, cultural pressures to have problems diagnosed, and the degree of availability of functional alternatives.

Antonovsky's model takes account of the fact that medical care constitutes a small social system that may be used to deal with diffuse social and psychological needs when the system is available, when its use is socially encouraged, and when it is receptive to people's needs and orientations. One study examining some aspects of this model in Israel, which has a population with high social need and a high physician-patient ratio, found that higher levels of need for catharsis, legitimation of failure, and the resolution of the magic-science conflict were associated with higher levels of utilization (Shuval, 1970). Another study in Israel by Mann and his colleagues (1970) found that latent social need was influential in the long-term pattern of use of health services. Persons who had been in concentration camps had much higher levels of utilization over a period of years that could not be accounted for solely on the basis of illness patterns.

The research on social need points to the fact that the provision of medical care is not simply an economic process, but also is an important aspect of social adaptation. We have ample evidence that there is large overlap between the occurrence of illness in populations that does not result in utilization of the physician and the most common presenting complaints seen by the physician of first contact. The main task for the behavioral scientist is to understand why persons with similar complaints behave so differently and why the same person with comparable symptoms at varying times chooses to seek medical care on one occasion but not on another (Mechanic, 1978a). Such processes depend on a wide range of factors, as the medical sociology literature suggests, including the organization of physician services and the receptivity of health personnel to varying types of problems and to sociocultural alternatives to medical care. Unfortunately, the large-scale utilization studies are not helpful in elucidating these processes. A much more careful dissection is required of the ways in which people perceive their bodies, make sense of their symptoms, and come to depend on the medical care system.

A variety of tentative models have been suggested (Zola, 1964; Rosenstock, 1969; Leventhal, 1970; Becker, 1974; Mechanic, 1978a). These models take into account the relationships between perceptions of illness and social functioning needs as well as such issues as attribution of cause and risks and benefits of treatment. Although these models direct attention to more subtle processes of perception and definition, they are difficult to test in large-scale cross-sectional surveys. These models thus tend to be examined in only one aspect or another, making it difficult to establish the degree of redundancy between different types of predictors described in the literature. In the future it would be useful to examine these psychosocial hypotheses concerning utilization, but in a context in which enabling variables are also taken into account, such as access to care, the availability of regular providers, and scope of insurance coverage. Examining the role of cultural and social-psychological processes within the constraining influences of economic and organizational factors will result in better theory and more adequate prediction.

Determinants of Illness Behavior

There are dramatic social and cultural differences in the way individuals and groups define illness and respond to symptoms. Moreover, the types of beliefs individuals have shape their responses to treatment and their cooperation with varying types of professionals. Successful treatment requires gaining the confidence of the patient, and this implies at least that the approach to treatment is not inconsistent with important social and cultural assumptions of the patient. The role of cultural differences in illness behavior is nicely illustrated by the classic study of Zborowski (1952) who described ethnic variations in responses to pain. He noted that while Jewish and Italian patients responded to pain in an emotional fashion, tending to exaggerate pain experiences, "Old Americans" tended to be more stoical and "objective," and Irish patients frequently denied pain. In addition, although Jews and Italians had similar manifest responses to pain, their underlying attitudes tended to be different. While the Italian patients sought relief from pain and seemed satisfied when relief was obtained, the Jewish patients seemed more concerned about the significance of their pain for future health. Thus pain medication might be more effective in the former case, and reassurance about future health in the latter case.

Suchman (1964), in a study of 5,340 persons from diverse ethnic groups in New York City, found that ethnocentric and socially cohesive groups included more persons who knew little about disease, were skeptical toward professional medical care, and reported a dependent pattern when ill. A more recent study of a Mormon population in Utah suggests, however, that an ethnocentric and socially cohesive group that supports the use of modern medicine may encourage high acceptance and high use of medical services (Geersten et al., 1975). The conclusion that one can draw from these studies is that cohesive group structures have considerable influence on members' behavior and can either assist or retard the treatment process.

Acquisition of Health Attitudes and Behavior—The wide range of variations in health and illness behavior from one culture to another and among varying ethnic groups suggests that, for the most part, these are learned differences. However, we understand relatively little about how these patterns are taught and acquired and how the health education of children can be altered successfully. In trying to explain the cultural differences he observed, Zborowski (1952) reported that Jewish and Italian patients related that their mothers showed overprotective and overconcerned attitudes about the children's health and participation in sports, and that they were constantly warned to avoid colds, fights, and other threatening situations. Zborowski suggested that this overprotective attitude fostered complaining and anxieties about illness. Schachter (1959) found that first-born and only children were more likely than others to want to be in the presence of another person when facing stress in adult life. Schachter hypothesized that the attention given to the first child and the inexperience of the parents in child rearing are likely to foster a greater dependence in such children compared with later-born children. Consistent with Schachter's hypothesis, Tessler (1980) found in a study of 1665 children from 587 families that early-born children were more frequent users of physician services than later-born, even controlling for variation in family size.

However simple the notion of cultural acquisition of illness behavior may appear, it is difficult to demonstrate empirically the processes of transmission. Mechanic (1964), using data acquired in 1961 from 350 children, their mothers, teachers, school records, and family illness diaries, found that the best predictors of children's illness responses were sex and age. By the fourth grade, girls were more likely to express pain and fear than boys, and these differences increased with age, although both older boys and girls were more stoical than younger children. Although the mothers' illness behavior patterns were predictive of decisions they made about the children's health, they did not successfully predict the children's response patterns in 1961.

I have now completed a 16-year follow-up of these children and have examined the developmental antecedents of a variety of health and illness responses and behaviors protective of or injurious to health (Mechanic, 1978b). One of the response patterns analyzed is a seven-item scale (alpha = 0.83) measuring the respondents' tendency to limit activities when they have various symptoms and their inclination to continue with usual activities when ill. Four childhood variables account for 8 percent of the variation in adult response: the mothers' reports 16 years earlier that they limited their usual work obligations when they had various symptoms (beta = 0.17); fewer days absent from school in 1960 (beta = −0.13); mothers scoring low 16 years earlier on a scale of personal control over illness (beta = −0.13); and the mothers' belief that risks were necessary (beta = 0.14). These predictors provide support for the assumption that sick-role behavior is in part learned in family contexts during childhood although the picture that emerges is complex and somewhat confusing. Other important predictors measured in young adulthood of the tendency to limit activities included a high level of concern with health, a higher tendency to complain about symptoms, less positive assessment of one's health, greater unhappiness, a lesser willingness to take risks, and higher skepticism of doctors and medical care. These correlates, added to the earlier predictors, explain one-fifth of the variance. The pattern of associations suggests that seeking release is in part learned, in part a reflection of discontent, and in part a product of a cautious orientation to self. The data are consistent with theoretical conceptions of sick role behavior that view such behavior as related to a desire to avoid adverse life situations, but also suggest that such behavior is complex and shaped by many factors.

Vocabularies of Distress—Social learning affects the vocabularies people use to describe their problems and complaints. It is reasonable to anticipate that persons from origins in which the expression of symptoms and a desire for help are permissible will be more likely to voice such feelings than those who are socialized in cultural settings that encourage denial of such feelings. Moreover, social groups differ in the extent to which they use and accept psychological and psychodynamic vocabularies, and these are likely to shape the way people conceptualize and deal with their distress. Kadushin (1969) found, for example, that persons who were receptive to psychotherapy were part of a loose social network of friends and supporters of psychotherapy. They shared the same life styles, liked the same music, and had in common many social and political ideas. Such networks tend to support and encourage psychological conceptualizations of problems just as certain families do. In contrast, other families and subgroups disapprove of such patterns of expression and tend to sanction them. Zborowski (1952), for example, in describing the "Old American" family stressed the tendency of the mother to teach the child to take pain "like a man," not to be a sissy, and not to cry. Such training, he argued, does not discourage use of the doctor, but implies that such use will be based on physical needs rather than emotional concerns.

It might be anticipated that persons from subgroups that discourage the expression of psychological distress will be inhibited from showing such distress directly, but will mask it with the presentation of more acceptable symptoms. Kerckhoff and Back (1968), in a study of the diffusion among women employees of a Southern mill of a hysterical illness alleged to be caused by an unknown insect, found that the prevalence of the condition was high among women under strain who could not admit that they had a problem and who did not know how to cope with it. Bart (1968), in comparing women who entered a neurology service but who were discharged with psychiatric diagnoses with women entering a psychiatric service of the same hospital, found that they were less educated, more rural, of lower socioeconomic status, and less likely to be Jewish. Of these women, 52 percent had had a hysterectomy as compared with 21 percent of women on the psychiatric service. Bart suggests that such patients may be expressing psychological distress through physical attributions, thus exposing themselves to unnecessary medical procedures.

Illness Behavior as a Means of Coping—It has already been noted that psychological distress increases the probability of medical care use. Illness behavior is part of a socially defined status and may serve as an effective means of achieving release from social expectations, as an excuse for failure, or as a way of obtaining a variety of privileges including monetary compensation. Moreover, the physician and other health personnel may be an important source of social support and may be particularly important for patients lacking strong social ties. A vague complaint of illness may be one way of seeking reassurance and support through a recognized and socially acceptable relationship when it is difficult for the patient to confront the underlying problem in an unambiguous way without displaying weaknesses and vulnerabilities contrary to expected and learned behavior patterns. Balint (1957) and others have noted that the presenting symptoms may be of no special importance, but serve to establish the relationship between the patient and the doctor.

There are many ways in which adaptive needs interact with

responses to symptoms and illness. A vast number of doctor–patient contacts involve symptoms and illnesses that are widely distributed in the population and that are more frequently untreated than treated (White et al. 1961). Thus the decision to seek care is frequently a result of contingencies surrounding the perception of symptoms. Perceptions of oneself as being ill and seeking care may provide self-justification when potential failure poses much greater symbolic threats to the person's self-esteem than do the process of being ill or dependent (Cole and Lejeune, 1972).

A related issue is the difficulty some patients have in differentiating between symptoms of psychological origin and those of particular diseases. Many illnesses or medications prescribed for dealing with them produce feelings that are comparable to those associated with stress and psychopathology. Such symptoms as fatigue, restlessness, and poor appetite, for example, may result either from depression or from an acute infectious disease. When both occur concurrently, patients may attribute the effects of one to another. There is indication, for example, that long convalescence from acute infectious disease may result from the attribution of symptoms caused by depression to the acute condition (Imboden et al., 1961). This complicates not only the patient's recovery but also the physician's perception and management of the patient.

Factors Affecting Symptom Definition and Patient Response—There is a wide variety of influences affecting the way people evaluate and make decisions with respect to their symptoms (Mechanic, 1978a). It is useful to classify these although the categories overlap to some degree. Three categories describe the characteristics of the symptoms: their visibility or recognizability, their frequency of occurrence, and the extent to which they are amenable to varying interpretive schemes. Symptoms that are frequent or occur visibly are more likely to be identified and result in some tangible response. Although some symptoms are only amenable to an illness interpretation (such as a high fever or an acute and persistent chest pain), other symptoms such as feeling depressed may be interpreted as a religious, social, or medical issue. Similarly, while some physical symptoms allow for varying possible hypotheses about cause and seriousness (such as fatigue or poor appetite), others do not. Two variables define the person's estimate of the impact of symptoms: perceived seriousness and extent of disruptiveness. Although physicians ordinarily focus on symptoms that are serious in their implications for future health, patients focus more often on symptoms that interfere in some obvious way with usual routines.

There are three classes of variables that define the person and his or her evaluative process: tolerance thresholds; the information, knowledge, understanding, and cultural assumptions of the evaluator; and the extent to which his or her needs interfere with an acceptance of an illness definition. People seem to vary a great deal in their subjective response to pain and discomfort, although there appears to be much less difference in physical thresholds. Much research has demonstrated that pain has an important subjective component, and there is no clear relationship between the amount of tissue damage and the degree of discomfort reported by the patient (Beecher, 1959). What people know, believe, and think about illness, of course, affects what symptoms they think are important, what is viewed as more or less serious, and what they should do. However, because of their social roles or personal desires, some persons deny illness. Often people wait until a convenient time to allow themselves to be ill and may ignore symptoms for long periods before taking action. There are some patients who have sufficient fear about particular illnesses or doctors so that they deny danger even when they fear they may have a particular disease such as cancer. These denial processes may be highly dysfunctional and result in more serious problems, but they appear to be deeply rooted in the individual's psychological responses (Janis and Mann, 1977). Such denial processes seem to be associated with high levels of fear but with inadequate defense and coping skills to deal with the degree of threat experienced. While threat motivates individuals to take action when they feel they can do something and know what to do, fear without sufficient coping capacity increases the chances of denial. An important function of health education is to short-circuit dysfunctional attribution and defensive processes in the face of illness threats and to provide individuals with more functional types of interpretations and pathways to effective response.

A final category of variables affecting illness behavior is the accessibility and social organization of the system of care itself. Practitioners tend to produce their own demand to some extent, and thus the level of use of ambulatory services, specialists, and beds depends on the number available (Fuchs, 1974). Moreover, ecological factors such as distance to care, and social accessibility factors such as availability of outreach, lack of stigma, and personal interest in the patient, all effect the patient's decision to come to services. Medical care is an iterative process; patients learn on the basis of their experience and the responses of health-care personnel how they are expected to use the system, and this may vary depending on the personnel and resources available and the views health-care personnel have of their social roles.

Developmental Aspects of Symptom Sensitivity: A Working Hypothesis—In my 16-year follow-up study of children, I have been examining the developmental aspects of reporting psychological distress in young adulthood (Mechanic, 1979). Using a seven-item scale comparable to those used in screening community populations for psychological disorder, I have been exploring how to interpret such distress reports and the appropriate way to conceptualize high levels of psychological pain as reported on such indices. Persons with such high generalized feelings of distress disproportionately come to physicians, psychiatric outpatient departments, counseling services, and social agencies.

Existing evidence indicate that such general distress measures reflect a range of problems. Some respondents with a high score on these scales are clearly patients with clinical disorders, but others are not. Dohrenwend (1980), in reviewing various interpretations of high scores on screening instruments, adopts Frank's (1974) concept of demoralization—a situation in which persons cannot meet environmental demands but cannot extricate themselves—to define what these instruments best measure. Among the factors acknowledged by Frank as contributing to demoralization are constitutional defects, environmental stresses, learned incapacity, existential despair, physical illnesses (especially chronic ones) and serious psychiatric symptoms. Dohrenwend finds this descriptive conceptualization consistent with his data.

While Frank suggests some factors likely to induce demoralization such as stress, learned incapacity, and physical illness, the manner in which these complex response patterns develop remains largely unknown. I have been investigating the hypothesis that high scores on psychiatric symptom scales reflect in part a complex pattern of illness behavior, preformed to some extent during childhood socialization and influenced over time by family experiences, adverse life events, coping responses, and available networks of social support. Although the findings from my 16-year longitudinal study are consistent with this model, the hypothesis still requires a great deal of empirical scrutiny. Below I review the basic assumptions of this hypothesis and some of the findings from the longitudinal study.

Perception of symptoms depends on changes in internal states, attention to such changes, and the cognitive meanings attributed to physical and psychological experience. Each of these three elements has its own determinants. Changes in internal states may result from biological changes, or the occurrence of illness or adverse life events, or failures in coping that cause psychophysiological arousal. Attention to internal feelings and a high level of self-awareness may result from early learning or experiences that focus people's attention on themselves or later experiences that induce an inner search for meaning. Meanings are acquired throughout life by cultural conditioning in the family, by exposure to peers, and through the mass media. The hypothesis argues that persons who learn to focus on internal changes because of developmental factors, who are exposed to adverse events and other life difficulties, and who define experiences so that they feel helpless and ineffectual are likely to report high levels of distress on psychiatric screening scales (Seligman, 1975). Although some such persons may suffer from such identifiable clinical disorders as a depressive syndrome, others primarily show an elaborate illness behavior response that has important learned components.

My study of children over a 16-year period indicates that those who had more frequent acute physical illnesses as children (such as colds, sore throats, and indigestion) and those who had more absence from school have greater psychological distress in young adulthood. While we cannot totally exclude the possibility of a constitutional explanation, or that children with more acute physical illness had more psychological distress in childhood, the data more closely support the hypothesis that children with more acute physical illness in childhood learn to focus on bodily sensations and that such self-awareness serves as a cognitive style affecting illness perceptions and response. In the adult follow-up, for example, we used a measure of introspectiveness indicating the extent to which respondents described themselves as introspective and sensitive, were worried about meaning in life, and were interested in psychology. Adult distress and the introspectiveness scale were associated 0.47.

Our data show that adulthood distress was also related to retrospective reports of parental behavior toward the child, situational stress in adulthood, and modes of handling emotion. For example, respondents who reported more negative behavior by parents toward them when they were growing up had more adulthood distress. One hypothesis is that such negative behavior is not only stressful and disorienting, but induces negative self-appraisal and internal monitoring which increases the probability of negative affect (Duval and Wicklund, 1972). Similarly, life stress induces higher levels of distress. Finally, inappropriate emotional management, such as "bottling up" feelings when angry, also contributes to distress. A variety of other predictors have been identified and are discussed elsewhere (Mechanic, 1979). I believe that such a cognitive developmental approach to understanding "distress syndromes" is promising, and requires a great deal of epidemiologic, developmental, and experimental work.

Implications for Health Care, Medical Research, and Medical Education

Illness behavior is a dynamic process through which the person defines the problems, struggles with them, and attempts to achieve a comfortable accommodation. Such processes of adaptation are partly learned and partly shaped by the social situation and influences in the immediate environment. The health worker thus can help guide the process by suggesting constructive alternatives for the patient and by avoiding the reinforcement of distorted meanings and maladaptive responses. Treatment personnel have considerable choice as to whether they encourage realistic understanding and coping efforts in their patients or whether they encourage dependence and helplessness. Often the medical care network has encouraged the patient to assume a dependent stance relative to the professional and has failed to support the patient's ability to struggle for mastery over his or her problems. The dependent stance is particularly evident in chronic illness in which the degree of social disability characterizing many patients far exceeds that required by the physical condition of the patient. While myocardial infarction patients, for example, may be troubled by the way their condition affects their ability to work and their family life, the physician frequently focuses too narrowly on minor variations in cardiac output (Aiken, 1976; Reif, 1975). Constructive illness behavior and the patient's coping capacities may influence outcomes to a greater degree than many of the physiological indicators on which physicians focus.

Illness behavior may seriously affect the way the physician comes to define the patient. The assessment of a patient's condition is more than a physical diagnosis; it is a construction of a comprehensive picture of events shaping the patient's reactions and it reflects not only evident physical symptoms and signs but also cultural patterns, peer pressures, self-identity, life difficulties, attitudes toward the value of medical care, and many other factors. Zola (1963), for example, studied a group of patients who were evaluated at various outpatient clinics at the Massachusetts General Hospital but for whom no medical disease was found. Zola found that psychogenesis was implied in the medical evaluation of 11 of the 12 Italian patients evaluated, but in only 4 of the 13 other cases. On the basis of a psychosocial study there was no evidence that the Italian patients had more life difficulties or psychological problems, but their mode of expressing distress was very different. Zola hypothesizes that the emotionality of the Italian patients, a cultural characteristic discussed earlier, was interpreted by the residents evaluating the patients as an indicator of psychiatric disturbance. Thus the behavioral pattern of expressing distress was confused with the patients' symptoms.

Much research in medicine and public health is based on populations selected from clinics, outpatient departments, and hospitals. Such populations, however, are the culmination of a selective flow determined not only by the nature, quality, and severity of the symptoms but also patients' sociocultural orientations and environmental pressures. Moreover, such populations are shaped by the special interests and attitudes of the personnel who operate these facilities, and they often select out patients of interest to them or with whom they most like to deal. Many such samples thus are highly biased representations of the population of patients with comparable illnesses, and attributions to the illness process that really reflect the biases of the sample are quite common. For example, it is frequently found that patients with particular diseases have high levels of stress, and it is often suggested that stress plays a role in the development of the condition. If stress, however, is an important factor triggering help-seeking, it is inevitable that treated populations will have higher stress levels than the population as a whole quite independent of any effect of stress on disease (Mechanic, 1963). Or, to cite another example, the factors sometimes identified as predictors of disease in treated populations are associated with seeking care from a particular type of practitioner, such as a psychiatrist, and are not necessarily related to either the particular disease state at issue or the help-seeking process in general. In researching particular populations of patients seeking care from a single source of care, one can mistakenly attribute to the illness process certain features of response characteristic of the particular pathway into care or place undue emphasis on the significance of particular symptoms (Shepherd et al., 1966).

Finally, illness behavior is an important consideration in planning medical education. The patients treated in teaching hospitals are highly selected populations of sick persons not only with respect to the types of illnesses they have, but also in terms of social and cultural factors that lead them to such care. Although many physicians are trained almost exclusively in such contexts, they will primarily have to work in more mundane settings in which the majority of patients have more limited problems. The strategies of approach to both health and illness must be different in these settings, and yet the models used for dealing with severe and acute illness are applied too commonly to patients with psychosocial problems, with chronic disabilities, and with self-limited acute illnesses. This results often in reinforcement of dysfunctional illness behavior and poor skills in coping. Recognition of the implications of illness behavior and social adaptation for health provides the young health professional and researcher with perspective in dealing with illness not only as an individual physiological affliction, but also as part of a social process.

Acknowledgments

This research was supported in part by grants from the Robert Wood Johnson Foundation and the Center for Epidemiologic Studies, National Institute of Mental Health. Portions of this chapter are taken from my book, *Medical Sociology*, 2nd ed., New York, Free Press, 1978.

References

Aday, L.A. & Andersen, R. (1975), *Development of Indices of Access to Medical Care*. Ann Arbor, Mich.: Health Administration Press.

Aday, L.A. & Eichhorn, R. (1972), *The Utilization of Health Services: Indices and Correlates. A Research Bibliography, 1972*. Rockville, Md.: National Center for Health Services Research and Development (DHEW Publication No. [HSM] 73-3003).

Aiken, L.H. (1976), Chronic illness and responsive ambulatory care. In: *The Growth of Bureaucratic Medicine: An Inquiry into the Dynamics of Patient Behavior and the Organization of Medical Care*, by D. Mechanic. New York: Wiley-Interscience, pp. 239-251.

Andersen, R., Kravits, J., & Anderson, O.W., eds. (1975), *Equity in Health Services: Empirical Analyses in Social Policy*. Cambridge: Ballinger Publishing Co.

Antonovsky, A. (1972), A model to explain visits to the doctor: with specific reference to the case of Israel. *J. Hlth Soc. Behav.*, 13:446–454.

Apple, D. (1960), How laymen define illness. *J. Hlth Hum. Behav.*, 1:219–225.

Balint, M. (1957), *The Doctor, His Patient and the Illness*. New York: International Universities Press.

Bart, P.B. (1968), Social structure and vocabularies of discomfort: what happened to female hysteria? *J. Hlth Soc. Behav.*, 9:188–193.

Baumann, B. (1961), Diversities in conceptions of health and physical fitness. *J. Hlth Hum. Behav.*, 2:39–46.

Becker, M.H., ed. (1974), *The Health Belief Model and Personal Health Behavior.* Thorofare, N.J.: Charles B. Slack.

Beecher, H.K. (1959), *Measurement of Subjective Responses: Quantitative Effects of Drugs.* New York: Oxford University Press.

Brown, G.W., Bone, M., Dalison, B., & Wing, J.K. (1966), *Schizophrenia and Social Care: A Comparative Follow-Up Study of 339 Schizophrenic Patients.* New York: Oxford University Press.

Cole, S. & Lejeune, R. (1972), Illness and the legitimation of failure. *Amer. Sociol. Rev.*, 37:347–356.

Dohrenwend, B.P., Shrout, P.E., Egri, G. and Mendelsohn, F.S. (1980), Nonspecific psychological distress and other dimensions of psychopathology. Archieves of General Psychiatry, 37:1229–1236.

Duval, S. & Wicklund, R.A. (1972), *A Theory of Objective Self-Awareness.* New York: Academic Press.

Eaton, J.W. & Weil, R.J. (1955), *Culture and Mental Disorders: A Comparative Study of the Hutterites and Other Populations.* Glencoe, Ill.: The Free Press.

Frank, J.D. (1974), *Persuasion and Healing: A Comparative Study of Psychotherapy*, New York: Schocken Books.

Fuchs, V.R. (1974), *Who Shall Live? Health Economics, and Social Choice.* New York: Basic Books.

Geertsen, R., Klauber, M.R., Rindflesh, M., Kane, R.L., & Gray, R. (1975), A re-examination of Suchman's views on social factors in health care utilization. *J. Hlth Soc. Behav.*, 16:226–237.

Glass, A.J. (1958), Observations upon the epidemiology of mental illness in troops during warfare. *Symposium on Preventive and Social Psychiatry.* Washington, D.C.: Walter Reed Army Institute of Research, U.S. Government Printing Office, pp. 185–198.

Greenley, J.R. & Mechanic, D. (1976), Social selection in seeking help for psychological problems. *J. Hlth Soc. Behav.*, 17:249–262.

Gurin, G., Veroff, J., & Feld, S. (1960), *Americans View Their Mental Health.* New York: Basic Books.

Imboden, J.B., Canter, A., & Cluff, L. (1961), Symptomatic recovery from medical disorders. *J. Amer. Med., Assn.*, 178:1182–1184.

Janis, I.L. & Mann, L. (1977), *Decision Making: A Psychological Analysis of Conflict, Choice, and Commitment.* New York: Free Press.

Kadushin, C. (1969), *Why People Go to Psychiatrists.* New York: Atherton.

Kasl, S.V. & Cobb, S. (1966a), Health behavior, illness behavior, and sick role behavior: I. health and illness behavior. *Arch. Environ. Hlth*, 12:246–266.

Kasl, S.V. & Cobb, S. (1966b), Health behavior, illness behavior, and sick-role behavior: II. sick-role behavior. *Arch. Environ. Hlth*, 12:531–541.

Kerckhoff, A.C. & Back, K.W. (1968), *The June Bug: A Study of Hysterical Contagion.* New York: Appleton-Century-Crofts.

Kohn, R. & White, K.L., eds. (1976), *Health Care—An International Study: Report of the World Health Organization/International Collaborative Study of Medical Care Utilization.* London: Oxford University Press.

Leventhal, H. (1970), Findings and theory in the study of fear communications. In: *Advances in Experimental Social Psychology*, ed. L. Berkowitz. New York: Academic Press, 5:119–186.

Lewis, C.E., Fein, R., & Mechanic, D. (1976), *A Right to Health: The Problem of Access to Primary Medical Care*, New York: Wiley-Interscience.

Lewis, C.E. & Lewis, M.A. (1977), The potential impact of sexual equality on health. *New Eng. J. Med.*, 297:863–869.

Lewis, C.E., Lewis, M.A., Lorimer, A., & Palmer, B.B. (1975), *Child-Initiated Care: A Study of the Determinants of the Illness Behavior of Children*. Los Angeles: University of California, Center for Health Sciences, unpublished report.

Maddox, G.L. (1962), Some correlates of differences in self-assessment of health status among the elderly. *J. Gerontol.*, 17:180–185.

Mann, K.J., Medalie, J.H., Lieber, E., Groen, J.J., & Guttman, L. (1970), *Visits to Doctors*. Jerusalem: Jerusalem Academic Press.

Mechanic, D. (1963), Some implications of illness behavior for medical sampling. *New Eng. J. Med.*, 269:244–247.

Mechanic, D. (1964), The influence of mothers on their children's health attitudes and behavior. *Pediatrics*, 33:444–453.

Mechanic, D. (1976a), *The Growth of Bureaucratic Medicine: An Inquiry into the Dynamics of Patient Behavior and the Organization of Medical Care*. New York: Wiley-Interscience.

Mechanic, D. (1976), Sex, illness, illness behavior, and the use of health services. *J. Hum. Stress*, 2:29–40.

Mechanic, D. (1976b), Stress, illness, and illness behavior. *J. Hum. Stress*, 2:2–6.

Mechanic, D. (1977), Illness behavior, social adaptation, and the management of illness: a comparison of educational and medical models. *J. Nerv. Ment. Dis.*, 165:79–87.

Mechanic, D. (1978b), Correlates of health and illness behavior: results from a 16-year follow-up study. Department of Sociology, University of Wisconsin: unpublished manuscript.

Mechanic, D. (1978a), *Medical Sociology*, 2nd ed. New York: The Free Press.

Mechanic, D. (1979), Development of psychological distress among young adults. Archives of General Psychiatry, 36:1233–1239.

Reif, L.J. (1975), *Cardiacs and Normals: The Social Construction of a Disability*, Ph.D. dissertation, University of California-San Francisco.

Robinson, D. (1971), *The Process of Becoming Ill*. London: Routledge and Kegan Paul.

Rosenstock, I.M. (1969), Prevention of illness and maintenance of health. In: *Poverty and Health: A Sociological Analysis*, ed. J. Kosa, A. Antonovsky, & I.K. Zola. Cambridge: Harvard University Press, pp. 168–190.

Schachter, S. (1959), *The Psychology of Affiliation: Experimental Studies of the Sources of Gregariousness*. Stanford: Stanford University Press.

Seligman, M.E.P. (1975), *Helplessness: On Depression, Development, and Death*. San Francisco: W.H. Freeman.

Shepherd, M., Oppenheim, A.N., & Mitchell, S. (1966), Childhood behavior disorders and the child-guidance clinic: an epidemiological study. *J. Child Psychol. Psychiat.*, 7:39–52.

Shuval, J.T. (1970), *Social Functions of Medical Practice*. San Francisco: Jossey-Bass.

Suchman, E.A. (1964), Sociomedical variations among ethnic groups. *Amer. J. Sociol.*, 70:319–331.

Tessler, R. (1980), Birth order, family size, and children's use of medical services: a research note. J. of Health Services Research 15:55–62.

Tessler, R. & Mechanic, D. (1978), Psychological distress and perceived health status. *J. Hlth Soc. Behav.* 19:254–262.

Tessler, R., Mechanic, D. & Dimond, M. (1976), The effect of psychological distress on physician utilization: a prospective study. *J. Hlth Soc. Behav.*, 17:353–364.

Ware, J.E., Jr., Davis-Avery, A., & Donald, C. (1978), *Conceptualization and Measurement of Health for Adults in the Health Insurance Study: Vol. V, General Health Perceptions*, Santa Monica, Calif.: Rand Reports R-19871 5-HEW.

White, K.L., Williams, T.F. & Greenberg, B.G. (1961), The ecology of medical care. *New Eng. J. Med.*, 265:885–892.

Wolinsky, F.D. (1978), Assessing the effects of predisposing, enabling, and illness-morbidity characteristics on health service utilization. *J. Hlth Soc. Behav.*, 19:384–396.

Zborowski, M. (1952), Cultural components in responses to pain. *J. Soc. Iss.*, 8:16–30.

Zola, I.K. (1963), Problems of communication, diagnosis, and patient care: the interplay of patient, physician and clinic organization. *J. Med. Ed.*, 38:829–838.

Zola, I.K. (1964), Illness behavior of the working class: implications and recommendations. In: *Blue-Collar World: Studies of the American Worker*, ed. A.B. Shostak & W. Gomberg. Englewood Cliffs, N.J.: Prentice-Hall, pp. 350–361.

Uses and Abuses of the Langner Index: A Reexamination of Findings on Psychological and Psychophysiological Distress

BLAIR WHEATON

The Langner Index has been one of the cornerstones of social, epidemiologic, and clinical research on mental health since its introduction in 1962 (Langner, 1962). The Index consists of the 22 symptoms, selected from a list of 120 characteristic psychiatric symptoms, which best distinguished between a "known-well" group and a "known-ill" group from Langner's research in midtown Manhattan. The problems surrounding the interpretation and use of this Index are the focus of this chapter.

Table 1 lists the 22 items in paraphrased form, and categorizes them according to four subgroups based on ratings by a sample of psychiatrists and internists (Crandell and Dohrenwend, 1967). The groupings reflect the varying nature of the included symptoms. One subgroup is made up of *psychological* symptoms which were seen as more psychological than physiological in nature and also were rarely indicative of organic disease. A second subgroup was labeled *psychophysiological* because, although the symptoms were seen as indicative primarily of psychological problems, they could be considered psychophysiological based on criteria in the Diagnostic Manual of the American Psychiatric Association used at the time. A third group of symptoms were rated as *physiological* because they most frequently indicated physical illness; and a fourth group of symptoms was simply labeled *ambiguous*, referring to the lack of agreement among the clinicians in Crandell and Dohrenwend's study as to what they indicated.

Why is it necessary to raise the already widely discussed conceptual and measurement issues surrounding the Langner items again? A good deal of criticism directed at these items has accumulated over the years (e.g., Manis et al., 1963; Dohrenwend and Dohrenwend, 1969; Phillips and Clancy, 1970; Seiler, 1973) leaving in some doubt the interpretation of substantive findings using the Langner Index. Despite this, the use of this Index, or parts of it, has persisted in published research. There is little need to provide an inventory of findings here, but it seems important to point out that even in recent years Langner items continue to be used in research on life-change events, the demographics of mental health, help-seeking and professional utilization, social support, and a range of other topics (Greenley and Mechanic, 1976; Singer et al., 1976; Tessler et al., 1976; Mueller et al., 1977; Wildman and Johnson, 1977; Carr and Krause, 1978; Micklin and Leon, 1978; Wheaton, 1978; Thoits and Hannan, 1979).

There is still need for clarification of what the Langer symptoms do and do not measure. The impression has been left that the Langner Index cannot be used to measure psychiatric disorder, that in any case it is riddled with response bias problems, that it is confounded with physical health problems, and that at best it can be considered a measure of general psychological and/or psychophysiological distress. The Langner Index is no more *just* a measure of distress than it is a comprehensive measure of mental illness.

In this chapter a middle-ground interpretation of the Langner Index will be suggested by taking advantage of differences in the subgroups of symptoms, particularly the psychological and the psychophysiological symptoms. Three interrelated issues will be addressed. First, there have been few attempts to define specifically the conceptual domain covered by the Langner Index. The various labels attached to this measure are a testimony to its conceptual vagueness. Practically every combination from a pool of adjectives including "psychological," "mental," "emotional," and "psychophysiological," and a pool of nouns including "impairment," "distress," "stress," "adjustment," "disturbance," and "disorder" has been used (Seiler, 1973). Many of the problems in interpreting results using the Langner Index can be traced to the absence of a specific description of what it is supposed to do. Second, there are a number of alleged measurement problems with these items that need to be examined more carefully. My claim is that the evidence against the Langner Index is not as damaging as it may appear at first. Third, if this is true, it is relevant to demonstrate how various subparts of the Index may be related to measures of physical health problems and specific psychiatric diagnoses. Data will be presented in the final section of the chapter that will allow for some preliminary conclusions about the degree to which the different subscales of the Index are con-

TABLE 1

The Four Subgroups of Symptoms from the Langner Index, According to Crandell and Dohrenwend (1967)

Psychological

1. Periods of days, weeks, months, when I can't get going.
2. Low spirits most of the time.
3. Periods of great restlessness.
4. Worrying type.
5. Nervousness (irritable, tense).
6. Trouble sleeping.
7. Memory not all right.
8. Feel somewhat apart even among friends.
9. Nothing ever turns out right.
10. Wonder if anything is worthwhile anymore.

Psychophysiological

[a]11. Feel weak all over most of the time.
[a]12. Suddenly feel hot all over.
[a]13. Bothered by cold sweats.
[a]14. Personal worries that get me down physically.
[a]15. Frequent headaches.

Physiological

[a]16. Poor appetite.
[a]17. Frequent fainting.
[a]18. Fullness or clogging in head much of the time.

Ambiguous

[a]19. Heart beats hard often.
[a]20. Shortness of breath without exercise.
[a]21. Acid stomach several times a week.
[a]22. Bothered by trembling hands often.

[a] Judged psychophysiological in nature using the 1952 Diagnostic and Statistical Manual of the American Psychiatric Association.

founded with physical illness and are effective predictors of the chances of having a psychiatric disorder.

Conceptual and Definitional Issues

An inherent assumption in much clinical work is a presence/absence notion of illness. This is probably not necessary for research purposes. It is at least safer to begin with a more continuous "degree of caseness" or "number of fulfilled necessary conditions" notion of illness that allows for a richer sense of variance in the phenomenon than to assume a dichotomy as given. It is still possible to collapse continuous notions into dichotomous ones for clinical and applied purposes; at the same time, the researcher is not losing the potentially useful information contained at the atomistic level of the raw symptoms. Certainly most researchers are ultimately interested in multiple-factor explanations of illness. It is instructive to note that multivariate prediction of dichotomous dependent variables often involves the use of statistical methods that treat the dependent variable as a likelihood or a probability of the presence rather than absence of a phenomenon, thereby introducing a continuous conceptualization of what is being predicted (e.g., log-linear models, logit regression models). Even to begin to think of multiple causation of illness, it is necessary to find a way to assign relative roles to predictors, and this in turn requires thinking about the dependent variable in more continuous terms than is allowed for by a dichotomy.

Symptom scales like the Langner Index can be useful for producing interval measures of the extent of a particular type of symptomatology. If it is possible for research purposes to allow for a direct translation from symptom scores to the *chances* of having specific psychiatric disorders, it is also possible to avoid endless—and ultimately artificial—controversies about cutting-points distinguishing between "wellness" and "illness" on symptom scales. Any definition of what the Langner items measure should explicitly recognize the dimensional nature of symptom indices. This does not, however, render such indices irrelevant to the measurement of diagnostically specific disorders. What is necessary is specification of the type of symptomatology most effectively measured by the index.

Langner himself pointed out that the items in the Index do not tap content associated with brain-related disorders or mental retardation. It is also clear that the symptoms shown in Table 1 do not tap schizophrenic or other psychotic behaviors (although some symptoms could be considered precursors or weak forms of psychotic symptoms). There is also a notable absence of the specifics necessary to measure personality disorders and sociopathic behavior.

The more physiological symptoms on the scale could be related to any of a number of psychophysiological reaction patterns, such as skin rashes, muscle pain, asthma, musculoskeletal reactions, stomach ulcers, constipation, and colitis (Coleman, 1964). The question is whether it is proper to represent psychophysiological symptoms as simply indicative of psychophysiological reactions, or more indirectly, as basic psychological states. The two most consistent themes running through the psychological and psychophysiological symptoms in Table 1 are depression and generalized anxiety. The psychophysiological symptoms may measure *both* underlying physical health problems and underlying anxiety or depression; it is more likely that the psychological symptoms measure more centrally an anxiety/depression syndrome.

It is unrealistic to expect the Langner symptoms to tap a broad range of severe symptomatology effectively. The type of anxiety and depression measured by the Langner symptoms is, on the other hand, probably not unrelated to clinical depression and anxiety. Assuming that the anxiety or depression measured by the Langner Index and clinical anxiety or depression are simply different phenomena may be ultimately misleading about the state of the findings on mental health at this point. A reasonable assumption is that scales like the Langner Index measure a range of symptomatology from none to moderately severe at best, but that the range is sufficient for such scales to be considered proxy measures of certain disorders.

One of the most widely used terms in interpreting the conceptual domain of the Langner Index is "impairment," implying a "discrepancy between the actual and potential capacity for performance" (Schwab et al., 1970, p. 55). The problem of inferring impairment from symptoms is one of assuming that a set of symptoms in fact has consequences for inhibition of potential. Ultimately, there is a value judgment here, but this is unavoidable if we are to be explicit. Conceptions of impairment are inevitably tied to perceptions of how *most* people function effectively. This statement implies that for some people certain symptoms will not have impairment connotations, but it is unlikely that this will be uniformly so when symptoms are added into scales. The problem might be conceptualized better as one of random measurement error in the items.

In sum, the Langner Index can be interpreted to refer to the extent of anxiety and depression symptomatology manifested by an individual, indicating an affectively based impairment in normatively defined social functioning capacities. The range of impairment is probably from none through moderate to lower levels of severe; this range is sufficient to make variation in scores on the Langner Index useful as a proxy indicator of variation in the probability of having enough impairment to qualify for a diagnosis within the realm of anxiety and depression disorders. Based on face validity only, it appears that the psychological symptoms on this scale operationalize this interpretation most effectively.

Measurement Problems

If we are to substantiate the claim that the Langner Index has the content referred to above, criticisms of its measurement adequacy must be answered. Four problems will be examined.

Reliability—Although not often reported, it is probably true that the Langner Index has moderate reliability. Summers et al. (1969) report an alpha coefficient of 0.75 for the full 22-item version of the Index using data from a cross-sectional sample of heads of household in two regions in Illniois. This is a reasonable, although not outstanding, level of reliability. Critiques of the Langner Index have paid little attention to the consequences of random measurement error. Such consequences need to be considered in interpreting findings in some of the validity studies of the Langner Index, especially those concerned with the persistence and stability of its symptoms over time. If the Langner symptoms are highly unstable, it would suggest that they are best interpreted only as immediate and self-limiting responses to a difficult environment. Stable symptoms, on the other hand, can be more readily interpreted as serious enough to be considered indicators of psychiatric disorder. Stability is usually measured by the degree of consistency of scores on a measure over time; the problem is that any demonstrated inconsistency can be due to random error in the measure as well as to instability of the phenomenon.

The interpretative complexities introduced by unreliability, however, need not be fatal. The researcher is really more interested in the true score on a measure than the observed score. The true score is often defined as the score that remains when the random error component is subtracted from the observed score. The relationship of a true score to an observed score can be thought of as analogous to the relationship between a factor and its constituent items in a factor analysis. Methods recently developed by Jöreskog and his colleagues (Jöreskog, 1973, 1976; Jöreskog and Sörbom, 1977) have made it possible, in effect, to estimate the consistency over time of the true-score factor underlying a set of symptoms rather than the consistency of the observed symptoms (see an example in Wheaton, 1978). Thus, stability can be estimated free of the effects of random error.

Validity—Various types of validity can be distinguished, although they are really different ways of approaching two basic validity questions: what does a measure measure and does it measure what we say it does? Content validity is established by demonstrating that the items on a particular measure are a sample of a universe of possible items for the concept in question (Cronbach and Meehl, 1955). The issue of content validity is problematic here, given that a content universe for the Langner Index has not been agreed upon (Dohrenwend and Dohrenwend, 1969). Whenever a content universe has not been clearly defined and no single, definite criterion measure exists that is acceptable for validation purposes, it is necessary to investigate the construct validity of a measure. This usually involves the use of a number of indirect criteria.

Questions about the validity of the Langner items surfaced in a study by Manis et al. (1963). Symptom scores were compared across five samples: a sample from the receiving wards of a mental hospital, a sample from the predischarge wards of the same hospital, a college student sample, and two community samples. Although the receiving ward sample had the highest mean Langner score, college students had the second highest, and the predischarge sample was tied with one of the community samples. This could be considered damaging evidence against validity (Seiler, 1973), but this result needs to be examined more carefully.

The description of the content of the Langner items offered in the previous section suggests one direct way of reinterpreting this finding. Patients in hospital settings are more likely to be there because of some form of "psychotic" rather than "neurotic" behavior. The Langner items do not measure psychotic symptomatology effectively but they probably pick up enough general impairment to elevate the scores of the receiving ward sample. The difference between the means of the predischarge group and the college student group is apparently not significant (assuming a two-tailed test). This lack of difference can be explained by three factors acting in combination: (1) any small to moderate differences in psychotic symptoms would not be measured well by the Langner Index; (2) the predischarge patients should be expected to be closer to the student and community samples in symptomatology than a receiving ward sample that has not yet undergone extensive treatment; and (3) it is reasonable to expect a college student sample to exhibit a fairly high rate of common neurotic symptoms, as Manis et al. (1963) themselves point out. Additional factors can be suggested. There may be numerous social selection processes affecting hospital release decisions which have the effect of leaving an unusually high proportion of relatively asymptomatic, but dependent, patients in a predischarge state. The other side of this coin is that we should not expect community respondents to be free of psychiatric disorders, especially the anxiety and depression disorders that are probably best measured by Langner scores. Weissman et al. (1978) report that it is exactly these diagnoses that are most prevalent in a recent study of urban community respondents.

Manis et al. (1963) also hypothesize that *all* patients in the receiving wards of the hospital should have higher symptom scores than patients in the predischarge wards. Because there is considerable overlap between the two distributions, the assumption is that this provides further damaging evidence to validity. The hypothesis itself sets up a "straw man." The fact that there is distributional overlap could reflect the effect of measurement error and nothing else. Moreover, there is no reason to assume there is no measurement error in the diagnosis and allocation decisions for patients, which is the ideal used to infer a lack of validity here.

A second study that questions the validity of the Langner items is that of Dohrenwend and Crandell (1970) on the behavior of various symptoms across four subgroups from the Washington Heights study. These subgroups consist of a sample of community leaders, a sample of heads of households, a sample of clinic outpatients in treatment, and a sample of hospitalized inpatients. Dohrenwend and Crandell do find that both patient samples have much higher median scores on the Langner Index than the community leaders or heads of household samples. The disturbing finding is that the outpatients have higher median scores than the inpatients. Dohrenwend and Crandell note: "We would hardly expect this to happen if this . . . measure provided an adequate index of the relative severity of disorder in the different groups" (p. 1613). Again, given that inpatients probably manifest more psychotic symptoms and fewer neurotic symptoms than outpatients (a contention consistent with the fact that schizophrenia is the single largest diagnostic category in institutionalized populations), the above finding seems more interpretable and somewhat less threatening. A plausible reason for the higher scores in the outpatient groups is the fact that the Langner measure is simply more sensitive to the types of symptoms manifested by outpatients.

Some studies do support the validity claims of the Langner Index. Volunteers in one study on psychotropic drugs were screened in an interview with a psychiatrist in order to remove individuals from the sample who exhibited "overt psychopathology" (Shader et al.,

1971). A number of paper-and-pencil measures were also administered, including the Langner scale. Women and men were interviewed at separate times and the data were analyzed separately. The psychiatrist was aware of each woman's test scores during her interview, but this was not true for men. Each of the three tests used—the Langner Index, a depression scale from the MMPI, and an anxiety scale—distinguished between accepted and rejected women for the study. However, only the Langner Index showed significantly different scores for accepted versus rejected men.

Stability—A related line of inquiry into the validity of the Langner items is concerned with the possibility that these items measure only transient psychological states and not the persistent types of symptoms usually associated with the concept of disorder. Dohrenwend and Dohrenwend (1969) have suggested that symptoms such as those on the Langner scale are sensitive to stressful events but also are often merely transient responses to such events. At the same time, the persistence of symptoms is believed to be one of the important indicators of clinical psychopathology (p. 107–108).

Two related problems have complicated studying the stability of symptoms. First, if we assume that groups of symptoms measure a common phenomen, it is more appropriate to investigate the stability of an index of such symptoms than the stability of individual symptoms. It is unreasonable to expect the individual symptoms on the Langner Index to be stable over time, especially when each symptom can be considered a functional equivalent of other symptoms on the scale. In such cases, an index should show greater stability than any of its constituent symptoms. The reason is that, when symptoms are added together, the random error in one item is being cancelled by the random error in another item or combination of items. This leads us to the second problem: not only are symptom indices more reliable measures of a phenomenon than are individual symptoms, but indices themselves also have some residual unreliability that needs to be taken into account. One way to do this is to posit that a single factor underlies a set of symptoms; when these symptoms are measured at two or more points in time, it is possible to estimate the correlation of the factor with itself at later points in time. This type of stability estimate is an improvement over those produced using symptom indices because, as noted earlier, the true score factor, and therefore the estimated correlation between factors, is formally free of random measurement error (Jöreskog and Sörbom, 1977).

Generally, the use of observed test-retest correlations to impute stability will result in underestimating the true stability of the Langner scale. Studies that report stability coefficients for Langner or related symptom scales provide evidence of a moderate level of stability, even with the effects of unreliability. Haberman (1965) studied the stability of Langner scores over a three-year period in New York City, and found a correlation of 0.54. This is interpreted as evidence of instability in the symptoms, but a balanced interpretation would suggest that this is evidence of some stability. Eaton (1978) reports a very similar stability of 0.55 over a two-year period in New Haven.

What happens when unreliability is taken into account? Assuming a single unobserved factor underlies the psychological and psychophysiological symptom subscales of the Langner Index, Wheaton (1978) estimated a stability of 0.67 and 0.75 in two separate samples in Illnois studied over a four-year period. There is an anomaly in this finding since Wheaton's samples are somewhat more rural than either Haberman's or Eaton's. But it is important to note as well that the four-year correlations for the two subscale measures are 0.31 and 0.53 in the first sample and 0.55 and 0.59 in the second sample. Thus, the true stability of the Langner Index may be somewhat higher than had been suggested previously.

Other evidence that the Langner Index measures relatively stable and persistent symptomatology is provided by Shader et al. (1971). The correlation between the Langner scale and an anxiety scale intended to tap stable anxiety was 0.773, while the correlation with an anxiety scale that measures short-term fluctuations in anxiety was a substantially lower 0.428. Taken together, these data suggest that the symptomatology measured by Langner scale scores is sufficiently stable to be interpreted as indicative of some types of psychiatric disorder. Of course, the most likely disorders are those that have moderate to moderately high stability.

Methods effects—The possibility has been suggested by a number of researchers that various types of "methods effects" are confounding interpretation of the Langner items as indicators of psychiatric disorder. Methods effects are present when characteristics of the measure or the measurement context partly determine responses to the measure. Dohrenwend and Dohrenwend (1969) identify at least four sources of possible distortion in responses to the Langner items: interviewer effects, acquiescence (yeasaying and naysaying), social desirability, and subcultural differences in expression and labeling of symptoms. A response bias in itself would not be damaging if the tendency were constant across respondents. A problem arises, however, when the response bias is also related to characteristics of the respondent that are potential predictors of symptomatology, such as socioeconomic status, ethnicity, sex, or age. This could lead to distorted and possibly spurious relationships between such variables and Langner scores.

The Dohrenwends do not produce evidence that interethnic or interracial interviewer effects or acquiescent response styles confound any relationships between Langner items and other variables. Phillips and Clancy (1970) measured naysaying by subtracting the number of yeasaying responses from a list of items that described psychologically or physically rare or impossible symptoms from the number of naysaying responses from a list of items which described "symptoms" common to everyone. Although naysaying was negatively related to Langner scores, there was no relationship between naysaying and the respondent's socioeconomic status. Thus, the evidence suggested naysaying did not confound the relationship between SES and Langner scores.

The most common methods-effect problem suggested has been the possibility that the respondent's tendency to admit to a symptom on the Langner Index is affected by his perception of the social undesirability of that symptom (Dohrenwend and Dohrenwend, 1969; Phillips and Clancy, 1970). Dohrenwend and Dohrenwend (1969) reported that social desirability conceptions of the Langner items do vary across ethnic groups: Puerto Ricans consistently rate these symptoms as less undesirable than Blacks, Jews, and Irish subgroups, and also have higher symptom rates. However, the interpretation of this result is complicated by the fact that Puerto Ricans may see the symptoms as less undesirable because they, in fact, do manifest more symptoms and therefore these symptoms are simply more common in their cultural milieu. It is not entirely clear from the Dohrenwends' data whether higher symptoms rates on the Langner measure are spurious because *all* they reflect is social desirability conceptions or whether they are real because there is a causal relationship between presence of symptoms and perceptions of their desirability. Without definitive data bearing on this question, we can at least conclude that the latter interpretation is sufficiently plausible to look for other evidence of confounding due to social undesirability effects.

Phillips and Segal (1969) hypothesized that sex differences in Langner scores may be partly due to the greater relative social desirability of these symptoms for women than men. But no direct ratings of the social desirability of the Langner symptoms are used in this study, and the authors themselves conclude that their data do not allow for an assessment of the effect of "real" sex differences versus male reluctance to admit to such symptoms.

Phillips and Clancy (1970) did measure respondents' perceptions of the social desirability of the 22 items on the Langner scale. The question was whether item desirability explained the inverse relationship between socioeconomic status and symptoms levels found in their data. Higher social desirability ratings were related to more reported symptoms, and social desirability was inversely related to SES, but desirability in itself did not account for the relationship between SES and symptoms. The relationship between SES and symptoms controlling for item desirability is attenuated, but is nevertheless still significant. The results, taken at face value, are therefore mixed: desirability conceptions have some influence, but not enough to obliterate the apparently real substantive relationship between SES and Langner scores. Three potential problems in interpreting the Phillips and Clancy data should be pointed out. First, they used education and income as measures of SES rather than an occupational status measure. A recent review of studies of social class and mental health (Fried, 1975) indicated that occupationally based measures of SES are the most common and that income may be the weakest indicator of SES in investigating relationships with psychiatric disorder. This puts the Phillips and Clancy data on uncertain ground in at least two respects. The SES index used makes the data less comparable with other studies than is desirable, and, moreover, the index incorporates an indicator (income) that may attenuate the relationship between SES and symptom scores to begin with. Second, there is a problem with the order of measures used in the interview. The Langner items were placed first in the interview. Admitting to a symptom could have affected the social desirability rating of that symptom, thereby inflating the relationship between desirability ratings and symptom scores. Finally, there is no way of telling whether or not the desirability ratings are related to different Langner subscale scores equally or are more related to some subscale scores than others. This issue is important because the differential validity of the subscales will be the focus of the ensuing discussion.

A number of potential sex-related biases in responding to the Langner items were measured by Clancy and Gove (1975). Although these data show that perceived undesirability, need for approval, and naysaying are all negatively related to the number of admitted symptoms, the most important finding is that men and women either do not differ on these sources of methods error (undesirability ratings and need for approval), or they differ in a direction that attenuates the observed relationship between sex and symptoms instead of inflating it (women are *higher* on naysaying and therefore tend to report fewer symptoms than they otherwise would).

The possibility of age-related response biases has been raised by Crandell and Dohrenwend (1967). The construct validity problem here, however, is that certain Langner items may be indicators primarily of physical rather than psychological illness and that this fact confounds interpretation of the relationships between other variables and the Langner Index.

The major source of this confounding with physical illness could be the psychophysiological group of items. Could these items be considered indicative of physical problems and thus result in spurious relationships between the Langner scale and age? Also, since the Langner Index has a number of psychophysiological symptoms, could the negative relationship between status and symptoms reflect the greater tendency among lower-status groups to express distress in somatic terms (Crandell and Dohrenwend, 1967)? Crandell and Dohrenwend report that the psychophysiological and ambiguous symptoms are related to age. This may or may not mean these subscales are especially confounded with physical illness; the matter will be investigated further in the next section. Both Crandell and Dohrenwend (1967) and Dohrenwend and Dohrenwend (1969) present data that is interpreted as suggesting that either lower-status groups or particular ethnic groups are more likely to express distress in somatic terms. This evidence is in the form of a "stronger" inverse relationship between education and the psychophysiological rather than the psychological symptoms in the first study, and a tendency for the significantly more symptomatic Puerto Ricans in the latter study to be especially elevated on levels of psychophysiological symptoms. There is also a significant (and "strong") inverse relationship both between psychological symptoms and education in the Crandell and Dohrenwend study, and between these symptoms and being Puerto Rican in the Dohrenwend and Dohrenwend study. Moreover, one cannot conclude from the statistical measures used in either study that relationships with the psychophysiological subscale are significantly more significant. This, at the least, suggests that relationships of the Langner Index with education, ethnicity, and other status-related variables are not hopelessly confounded with variation in rates of physical illness across sociodemographic groups.

The possibility that the psychophysiological and psychological subscales may operate differently as measures of physical versus psychiatric conditions needs to be examined more carefully. If this possibility is in fact the case, it will be necessary to be specific about which parts of the Langner Index can be safely considered indicators of psychiatric conditions. Data pertaining to this issue will be presented in the next section.

The Relationship between Langner Subscales and Measures of Physical and Psychiatric Disorder

Four hypotheses relevant to the interpretation of and use of the Langner items in research will be examined:

1. The psychophysiological symptoms are more confounded with physical illness problems than are the psychological symptoms.
2. The degree to which psychophysiological symptoms predict physical illness problems changes more across ethnic groups (in this case, Mexican versus Anglo groups) than the degree to which psychological symptoms predict physical illness problems.
3. The psychological symptom subscale predicts chances of a psychiatric diagnosis more efficiently than does the psychophysiological subscale.
4. The psychological symptom subscale is primarily related to chances of a diagnosis in the realm of anxiety and depression disorders, and is much less related to other types of diagnoses.

Hypotheses 1 and 2 were assessed using data from a comparative, cross-sectional study of social stressors and psychiatric symptoms among Mexican, Mexican-American, and Anglo adults in El Paso, Texas, and Juarez, Mexico, in 1975. In El Paso, dwellings were randomly selected from the city directory and one adult between ages 18 and 65 was randomly chosen in each household. In Juarez, a multistage area sample based on aerial photographs was used. Respondents were divided into four samples: (a) Anglos living in El Paso and raised in the United States, N = 132; (b) Mexican-Americans living in El Paso and raised in the U.S., N = 104; (c) Mexicans living in El Paso but raised in Mexico, N = 90; and (d) Mexicans living in Juarez and raised in Mexico, N = 133.

Besides containing all 22 symptoms from the Langner Index and a number of sociodemographic variables, these data also include measures of 42 physical symptoms. Respondents were asked how often each of the physical problems had occurred in the last twelve months. To make this information more manageable, a factor analysis of all 42 items was performed. This resulted in 14 indices combining various symptoms and nine separate problems that did not load highly on any factor. An overall Physical Problems Index was also created by counting a "fairly often" or "very often" response in reporting the frequency of each symptom as 1 and a "sometimes" or "never" response as 0, and summing across all 42 items.

The 14 indices used in the analysis that follows are described below:

1. Colds and Flu: sore throats, coughing, colds or flu, trouble swallowing, diarrhea.
2. Abdominal Pain (Women): severe menstrual troubles, trouble swallowing, abdominal pain, trouble urinating, sore muscles not related to exercise or work, stomach aches.
3. Stomach Problems: abdominal pain, stomach aches, vomiting.
4. Arthritic and Muscle Pain: arthritis, rheumatism, or bursitis, swollen arms and legs, sore muscles, difficulty walking.
5. Allergies: Skin Rashes: itching skin, skin rashes.
6. Seasonal Allergies: runny nose, sneezing, and itching of nose or eyes.
7. Breathing Problems: asthma attacks or wheezing, trouble breathing.
8. Menopausal/Vaginal Problems (Women): menopausal problems, vaginitis, trouble urinating, dizziness.
9. Elimination Problems: constipation, trouble urinating.
10. Feeling Rundown: bothered by all kinds of ailments (aches and pains) when nothing specific seemed to be wrong, getting tired easily, bleeding easily, looking pale.
11. Internal Bleeding: internal bleeding, abdominal pain.
12. Eye and Ear Problems: ears ringing, spots before eyes, earaches.
13. Fever: dizziness, stomach aches, chills, cold or flu symptoms.
14. Diabetes: diarrhea, nose bleeding, unusual thirst.

An interpretive approach to the grouping of symptoms in the factor analysis was taken whenever possible. For instance, "runny nose," "sneezing," and "itching of nose or eyes" loaded on a separate factor and did not load at all with cold or flu symptoms. As a result, these symptoms were interpreted as indicating allergy problems. The particular symptoms on the diabetes factor may be common among diabetics, but this does not mean we have a pure diagnostic measure of diabetes in these data. Rather, the approach was to label factors in order to be clear about what the symptoms might indicate. The factor labeled "Feeling Rundown" could just as easily have been labeled "Hypochondriachal Tendencies." The indices are not intended to be conceptually distinct; some symptoms are repeated in different indices. This is not a problem since these variables enter the analysis as a series of successive dependent variables. Nine separate symptom items were also retained: stomach ulcers, chest pains, diarrhea, constipation, backaches, unusual thirst, easy bleeding, varicose veins, and lumps in the body.

The 22 Langner items were also factor-analyzed to test for consistency with the Crandell and Dohrenwend classifications in Table 1. The most interpretable solution, both in the total sample and four separate samples, yielded three factors: psychological symptoms, ambiguous symptoms, and a combination of psychophysiological, physiological, and ambiguous symptoms. The overlap with the classifications in Table 1 was considerable. Three Langner indices were created from the results of the factor analysis, resulting in some modification of the subscales in Table 1. First, the psychological symptom scale did comprise a separate factor, with the addition of the "personal worries that get me down physically" item. Second, there was no justification for distinguishing between the psychophysiological symptoms and the purely physiological symptoms since they both loaded equally well on the same factor. Third, two of the ambiguous symptoms, "heart beats hard often" and "shortness of breath without exercise," loaded on a separate factor and were retained as a separate subscale. The other two ambiguous symptoms, however, loaded on the psychophysiological factor, and were included on that subscale.

A number of regression models were estimated with physical problem measures as dependent variables and the Langner subscales as independent variables. Of course, the causal direction may also be in the other direction, but the issue here is a measurement (not a causal) issue, and specifying models as above is sufficient for studying the issue of confounding. In general, the psychophysiological symptoms were substantially more correlated with the physical problem measures than either the ambiguous or the psychological symptoms. A rough indication of this fact is reflected by differences between subscales in their average correlation with physical problems: for the psychophysiological symptoms, the average correlation was 0.33, while for both the ambiguous and psychological symptoms it was 0.17. It is reasonable to expect some correlation between physical problems and the psychological subscale, since physical illness could be one cause of psychological distress.

The possibility that the Langner subscales were not equally confounded with physical problems across the four samples in this study was investigated first. Essentially there were two issues here: whether or not the psychophysiological symptoms were more or less confounded with physical problems in the Mexican groups than in the Anglo group; and whether or not the psychological symptoms were unconfounded with physical problems in all groups.

The Physical Problems Index was regressed on the three Langner subscales separately using the combined sample (N = 463). Dummy variables standing for subsample membership were added as a second step to each equation, and interactions between the symptom subscale in question and sample membership were added as a third step. There were significant interactions for the psychophysiological ($p < 0.01$) and ambiguous symptoms ($p < 0.05$), but no significant interaction involving the psychological symptoms. When all three Langner subscales were entered as predictors in the same model, and sample membership and all two-way interactions were added in succeeding steps, the interactions again produced a significant increment in explained variance in physical problems ($p < 0.01$).

It appears that the psychophysiological and ambiguous symptoms are the main sources of interaction here. To describe the nature of the interaction more specifically, regressions were run in each of the four separate samples with the three Langner subscales as predictors. Results for these models are shown in Table 2. It is clear that the psychophysiological symptoms are considerably more confounded with physical problems in the Mexican groups. This denotes a problem with any general application of the Langner Index: one cannot assume that the psychophysiological symptoms have the same meaning across ethnic groups. Not only may some groups express distress in more somatic terms (Dohrenwend and Dohrenwend, 1969), but the use of the psychophysiological symptoms is further complicated by the fact that these symptoms may be more confounded with physical illness in these same groups. These results also suggest that if one is interested in measuring psychiatric symptomatology and not physical illness in Anglos in the U.S., use of the psychological and psychophysiological subscales may be warranted, but the ambiguous symptoms are substantially confounded with physical illness problems.

The effect of the psychological symptoms is reasonably consistent across groups, with the exception of a barely significant coefficient among Mexicans in El Paso. Given the previous test for interaction

TABLE 2

Regression of Physical Problems Index on Langner Subscales in Four Samples from El Paso/Juarez Community Study

	Anglos		Mexican-Americans		Mexicans in El Paso		Mexicans in Juarez	
	b	β	b	β	b	β	b	β
I. Basic Model								
Psychophysiological	0.05	0.11	0.10[a]	0.38	0.15[a]	0.39	0.20[a]	0.51
Ambiguous	0.44[a]	0.34	0.12	0.15	0.17	0.14	−0.08	−0.06
Psychological	−0.00	−0.01	0.02	0.16	0.04[b]	0.21	0.03	0.15
R^2	0.15		0.27		0.33		0.34	
II. With Controls for sex, age, SES, and education added								
Psychophysiological	0.05	0.12	0.09[a]	0.36	0.14[a]	0.38	0.19[a]	0.49
Ambiguous	0.43[a]	0.34	0.08	0.10	0.19	0.16	−0.10	−0.07
Psychological	0.00	0.00	0.03	0.19	0.05[b]	0.23	0.04	0.15
R^2	0.17		0.33		0.35		0.36	

[a] $p < 0.01$.
[b] $p < 0.05$.

reported above, this cannot be interpreted as indicating a sufficiently strong difference across groups to warrant the conclusion that the psychological subscale has inconsistent effects. The main conclusions from Table 2 are that the psychophysiological symptoms are especially confounded with or, more accurately, indicative of physical illness among respondents of Mexican background, that the ambiguous symptoms are especially indicative of physical illness among Anglos, and that, if one is interested in avoiding this problem, the psychological symptoms on the Langner Index are the safest bet. These conclusions are unchanged when controls for sex, age, SES, and education are added to each model.

Table 3 shows a more detailed description of the relationships between Langner subscales and various physical problems. This analysis was conducted on the total combined sample, including controls for sample differences and sociodemographic factors. Because interactions with sample membership are excluded, these results stand for an "averaged" effect of the Langner subscales across groups. The most impressive result in Table 3 is the consistency with which psychophysiological symptoms predict a wide range of physical conditions. Only for one of twenty-three physical problem variables is the coefficient for psychophysiological symptoms nonsignificant. On the other hand, psychological symptoms are unrelated to physical problems in eighteen of twenty-three cases. Whatever correlation there is between psychological symptoms and physical illness problems seems to be most generally explained by the fact that psychological symptom scores are correlated with psychophysiological symptom scores ($r = 0.36$). What does this imply? Perhaps the psychophysiological symptoms are simply less specific in their content referents than the psychological symptoms: they could be considered indicators of both physiological and psychological distress.

Psychological symptoms are related to physical problems in five cases: arthritic or muscle pain, feeling rundown, internal bleeding, eye/ear problems, and varicose veins. In every case, the relationship could be plausibly explained by referring to the physical problem involved either as an indirect measure or as a cause of the same type of distress as that measured by these psychological symptoms. These problems often include diffuse and/or unobservable symptoms which could be considered closer in kind to the psychological symptoms on the Langner Index than the other more specific physical problems in Table 3. This applies most obviously to the "Feeling Rundown" index. The symptoms on this index are often considered to be psychosomatic in origin, or even indicative of

TABLE 3

Regressions of Physical Problem Items on Langner Subscales in Total Combined Sample, El Paso/Juarez Community Study, with Controls for Sample and Sociodemographic Differences Added, Standardized Coefficients Only

Dependent Variables	Psycho-physiological	Ambiguous	Psycho-logical
Cold/Flu	0.44[a]	0.01	0.03
Menstrual/Abdominal (Women)	0.47[a]	−0.03	0.11
Stomach Problems	0.44[a]	−0.04	0.08
Arthritic/Muscle Pain	0.22[a]	0.20[a]	0.15[a]
Allergies, Skin Rashes	0.23[a]	−0.03	0.09
Allergies, Seasonal	0.41[a]	−0.02	−0.04
Breathing Problems	0.24[a]	0.22[a]	−0.05
Menopausal/Vaginal Problems (Women)	0.19[a]	0.16[b]	0.08
Elimination Problems	0.29[a]	0.07	0.09
Feeling Rundown	0.40[a]	0.10[b]	0.13[a]
Internal Bleeding	0.28[a]	−0.02	0.12[b]
Eye/Ear Problems	0.27[a]	0.07	0.10[b]
Fever	0.50[a]	−0.02	0.02
Diabetic	0.28[a]	0.08	0.06
Stomach Ulcer	0.19[a]	−0.04	−0.04
Chest Pains	0.22[a]	0.32[a]	−0.02
Diarrhea	0.29[a]	0.04	0.02
Constipation	0.27[a]	0.07	0.05
Backaches	0.24[a]	0.07	0.08
Unusually Thirsty	0.17[a]	0.09	0.05
Easy Bleeding	0.16[a]	0.09	0.06
Varicose Veins	0.03	0.11[b]	0.14[a]
Lumps in Body	0.14[b]	0.06	0.01

[a] $p < 0.01$.
[b] $p < 0.05$.

general hypochondriachal tendencies. Muscle pain could also be interpreted in this way, but specific arthritic symptoms are more likely to be a cause of psychological symptoms than a measure of them. Thus, the "Arthritic and Muscle Pain" index may be related to the psychological subscale for both reasons suggested above. The fact that psychological symptoms accompany varicose veins, which are among other things an external cosmetics problem, is more readily understandable as an example of a simple cause-and-effect relationship. The two remaining problems—internal bleeding and eye/ear problems—deserve additional comment. Given that the psychological subscale has a residual effect on predicting physical problems in only five of twenty-three cases, there is the risk of over-interpreting these results. But it should be pointed out for both indicies that first, the relationship with psychological symptoms was barely significant at the 0.05 level, and second, some of the symptoms on the index are possibly stress-related and, under certain conditions, indicative of psychological problems.

These data point to the fact that the psychophysiological subscale of the Langner Index cannot be generally assumed to be indicative only of the types of symptoms that accompany psychiatric disorder. The interpretation of the Langner Index offered earlier may apply most specifically to the psychological symptoms on this Index, but this remains to be demonstrated.

To assess hypotheses 3 and 4, data from a three-wave panel study in New Haven were used. A baseline sample of 938 adults selected randomly within households was collected in 1967. The sample was obtained from a total population of 72,000, the catchment area of the local community mental health center. Follow-ups were conducted in 1969 (N = 720) and 1975 (N = 511). The data used here were collected on the 1975 sample. Although the 1967–1969 panel members were not sociodemographically different from attriters, there was a tendency over the 1969–1975 period to select out of the sample nonwhites and lower-SES subjects (Weissman et al., 1978). It is not clear whether this would affect the analyses reported here using psychiatric diagnoses, but it is always possible with attrition in panel samples that variance on some variables is attenuated. If this applied to the psychiatric diagnoses, for instance, leading to a lower proportion of subjects with a diagnosis than would otherwise occur without selective attrition, it could result in relationships between psychiatric diagnoses and Langner scores which would appear to be weaker than they really are.

Eighteen of the 22 Langner items were included at various places in the 1975 interview: nine of the ten psychological symptoms (excluding #9, Table 1), three of the five psychophysiological symptoms (excluding #12 and #14), two of the three physiological symptoms (excluding #18), and all of the ambiguous symptoms. A factor analysis of these items yielded three factors: a psychological symptom factor, a factor dominated by psychophysiological symptoms (but also including the two ambiguous symptoms which loaded on a separate factor in the previous data set), and a factor of mixed physiological and ambiguous symptoms, less amenable to interpretation. Indices were created from the first and second factors only.

Diagnostically specific measures of psychiatric disorder were developed from the Schedule for Affective Disorders and Schizophrenia, or SADS (Endicott and Spitzer, 1977), a structured interview schedule given in 1975 which contains a comprehensive assessment of functioning relevant for making diagnoses for the major psychotic, neurotic, and personality disorders. Subjects were classified as to diagnosis using the Research Diagnostic Criteria (Spitzer et al., 1977). Both current and lifetime diagnoses can be derived from the SADS interview. For current diagnoses, some of the categories are mutually exclusive and some are not. Thus, a small percentage of the sample (4.5%) is in more than one category of current diagnosis. More subjects (15% of the sample) have had multiple diagnoses over their lifetimes. This means that comparisons across diagnostic categories are not entirely independent. A number of diagnoses yielded very small numbers (equal to or less than 3 people) and were dropped from the present analysis. Because of the importance of comparing findings across diagnostic categories, however, some diagnoses with small numbers (4–8) had to be included. Since the findings yielded by these diagnoses make sense when compared to other more prevalent diagnoses, and it is only the pattern of findings across diagnoses that is important here, the inclusion of relatively rare diagnoses seems not only necessary, but justified.

In Tables 4 and 5 percentage distributions of respondents at each level of symptomatology on the two Langner subscales who also have various psychiatric diagnoses are shown. Table 4 shows distributions for the psychological subscale, Table 5 for the psychophysiological subscale. The psychological subscale was divided into five symptom levels and the psychophysiological subscale into four (the categories are as even in size as possible). Because of the more compact distribution of the psychophysiological scale, it was impossible to divide it into five categories. Also, because of the lower number with current diagnoses, findings for lifetime diagnoses are also presented in each table. This results in relationships between past diagnoses and current symptom levels, but this is allowable since we do not consider the relationships shown to be addressing substantive issues so much as measurement issues.

The distributions in Tables 4 and 5 are derived from a series of two-way tabulations of the presence or absence of a diagnosis by symptom level. For each row, the percent in each cell reflects the percentage of the total number of individuals at a given symptom level who have that particular diagnosis (the percentages for the absence of a diagnosis are of course the complement of those shown

TABLE 4

Percentage of Respondents in Psychological Symptom Categories with Selected SADS Psychiatric Diagnoses, New Haven Community Study

Diagnosis:	N	None	Psychological Symptom Level[a] Mild	Moderate	High	Very High	Sig. Level χ^2
I. Current							
Major Depression	22	0.0	0.8	2.2	3.4	27.1	0.00
Minor Depression	13	0.0	0.8	2.2	4.5	10.2	0.00
Generalized Anxiety	13	0.0	1.6	1.1	6.7	6.8	0.00
Alcoholic	12	0.7	2.4	3.3	3.4	3.4	0.60
Phobia	7	0.7	0.8	2.2	2.2	1.7	0.77
Any Diagnosis	88	2.8	8.8	13.3	30.3	56.7	0.00
Depression: Major or Minor	35	0.0	1.6	4.4	7.9	37.3	0.00
II. Lifetime							
Schizophrenic	4	1.4	0.0	1.1	0.0	1.7	0.54
Hypomania	4	0.7	0.0	0.0	1.1	3.4	0.14
Major Depression	100	7.7	14.4	22.2	28.1	44.1	0.00
Minor Depression	47	4.9	7.2	12.2	10.1	18.6	0.03
Panic Disorder	10	0.7	0.8	1.1	3.4	6.8	0.03
Generalized Anxiety	49	4.9	7.2	10.0	14.6	18.6	0.00
Depressive Personality	23	1.4	0.0	1.1	10.1	18.6	0.00
Alcoholic	33	3.5	5.6	5.6	12.4	8.5	0.10
Drug Abuse	8	0.7	1.6	1.1	2.2	3.4	0.67
Phobia	12	1.4	0.8	2.2	4.5	5.1	0.24
Any Diagnosis	207	22.4	32.0	43.3	53.9	80.0	0.00

[a]Symptom level categories reflect the division of the 506 respondents with data present into as equally sized categories as the distribution of scores would allow. The Ns for each category are: none = 143; mild = 125; moderate = 90; high = 89; and very high = 59.

TABLE 5

Percentage of Respondents in Psychophysiological Symptom Categories with Selected SADS Psychiatric Diagnoses, New Haven Community Study

Diagnosis	N	Psychophysiological Symptom Level[a] None	Mild	Moderate	High	Sig. Level χ^2
I. Current						
Major Depression	22	1.4	5.2	2.8	20.8	0.00
Minor Depression	13	1.1	3.1	5.6	5.7	0.06
Generalized Anxiety	13	1.1	4.1	4.2	5.7	0.09
Alcoholic	12	2.1	3.1	2.8	1.9	0.94
Phobia	7	1.1	2.1	1.4	1.9	0.88
Any Diagnosis	88	8.1	20.6	23.6	51.9	0.00
Depression: Major or Minor	35	2.5	8.2	8.3	26.4	0.00
II. Lifetime						
Schizophrenic	4	0.7	1.0	0.0	1.9	0.69
Hypomania	4	0.4	2.1	0.0	1.9	0.25
Major Depression	100	11.3	25.8	27.8	43.4	0.00
Minor Depression	47	5.6	13.4	16.7	11.3	0.01
Panic Disorder	10	1.4	2.1	1.4	5.7	0.23
Generalized Anxiety	49	8.1	12.4	6.9	17.0	0.14
Depressive Personality	23	1.4	6.2	6.9	15.1	0.00
Alcoholic	33	3.9	7.2	6.9	18.9	0.00
Drug Abuse	8	1.4	2.1	1.4	1.9	0.96
Phobia	12	1.8	3.1	2.8	3.8	0.76
Any Diagnosis	207	28.9	51.5	50.0	72.2	0.00

[a] Symptom level categories reflect the division of the 506 respondents with data present into as equally sized categories as the distribution of scores would allow. The Ns for each category are: none = 218; mild = 108; moderate = 102; and high = 78.

and are not reported in either table). The significance levels reported in each row are from the chi-square significance test for each crosstabulation.

The fact that the psychological subscale is more strongly and more consistently related to chances of having a psychiatric diagnosis than the psychophysiological symptoms can be inferred from the percentage distributions for "Any Diagnosis" in Tables 4 and 5. For current diagnoses, for instance, the psychological subscale is somewhat more discriminatory than the psychophysiological subscale. Just 2.8% of those with no psychological symptoms have a diagnosis—a figure small enough to be attributable to measurement error, while 56.7% of those in the highest psychological symptom category have a diagnosis. This is a difference of around 54% between the lowest and the highest category. The comparable range for the psychophysiological scale (Table 5) is about 44%, and 8.1% of those with no psychophysiological symptoms have a diagnosis. Note also that the rate of increase in percentage who have a diagnosis is more constant, and therefore more linear, for categories on the psychological subscale than for categories on the psychophysiological scale. This result generalizes to many of the diagnoses being compared here, and argues further for the greater utility of the psychological subscale.

Why is it that only 52–56% of those in the highest symptom categories have some current diagnosis? This is where a middle-ground interpretation is useful. It is of course true that a significant number in the highest symptom categories do not have a diagnosis. In the interpretation of the range of symptomatology measured by the Langner items discussed earlier, it was emphasized that the highest symptom levels probably tapped only moderately severe disorder at best. If the range could be extended, there probably would be higher proportions with a diagnosis in the highest symptom category. A reasonable interpretation is that, as it stands, the Langner Index does not measure the *full* range of chances of having a diagnosis, and this will result in it being a conservative indicator of relationships between certain variables and psychiatric disorder. At the same time, the psychological subscale measures a significant range of variation in chances of having a diagnosis, and this fact cannot be discounted.

It is important to point out as well that the percentage of those having a diagnosis in the high symptom level categories in both tables is related to the total number who have that diagnosis: the higher the N, the higher the percentage in the high symptom category who have that diagnosis. This denotes a simple fact: the fewer number of cases available for a diagnosis, the lower the absolute number available to be distributed across the symptom categories, and thus the lower the percentage in any category. What should be interpreted are the trends in the distributions more than the absolute magnitudes of the percentages.

Table 4 makes it clear that the psychological subscale is mainly related to the depression and anxiety disorders, whether current or lifetime. While level of psychological symptomatology predicts chances of receiving a diagnosis of major or minor depression, generalized anxiety, and panic disorder (lifetime), it is unrelated to alcoholism, phobia, drug abuse, schizophrenia (lifetime), and hypomania (lifetime). The Ns in the last two diagnoses are very small, but no pattern is present. This is less true of the psychophysiological subscale: it is not strongly related to chances of minor depression, and it is unrelated to the generalized anxiety and panic disorder diagnoses.

These results point to one central conclusion. The interpretation of the Langner Index developed in this chapter—that it measures a significant range in the probability of being diagnosed as having an anxiety or depression disorder and that it is not an invalid indicator of these disorders—seems to apply specifically to the psychological symptoms on this scale. These symptoms are factorially cohesive, they are not confounded with physical illness, and they predict chances of having the specified diagnoses. The psychophysiological symptoms on this Index are more problematic: their interpretation is more variable from group to group, they are often closely associated with physical illness, and they are not as strongly related to chances of receiving a psychiatric diagnosis. If one is interested in interpreting results with Langner symptoms in terms of psychiatric disorder, it is probably safest to use the psychological symptoms only.

These results also suggest that the kind of depression and anxiety measured by the Langner Index is not "qualitatively" different from clinical depression and anxiety; rather the difference is at most quantitative. If the types of symptoms tapped were qualitatively different, the relationships in Tables 4 and 5 should not have surfaced.

What does this discussion imply about the use of the Langner items in research? First, the Langner psychological symptoms have a specific interpretation in terms of the type of psychiatric symptomatology and range of impairment they measure. A specific conceptual domain needs to be defined before Langner items can be interpreted properly. Second, the evidence for the invalidity of these items is at best equivocal. Until better evidence is produced, these items deserve to be interpreted as valid indicators of psychiatric problems. Third, Langner symptoms have sufficient stability to be considered more than transient responses to stressful environments. Their stability is on a par with the level of persistence associated with clinical symptomatology, especially when applied to depression or anxiety disorders rather than schizophrenia. Fourth, the contention that the psychophysiological symptoms on this index may be measuring physical illness more than anything else must be taken seriously. Fifth, the psychological subscale is the most specific and most discriminatory measure of variation in chances of receiving a diagnosis of an anxiety or depression disorder, and should be used exclusively if one wants to maximize the chances of comparability of findings across populations. Finally, if a translation exists between psychological symptom scores and chances of receiving a psychiatric diagnosis, it has implications for current findings on the relationship between various sociodemographic factors and some types of disorder. Fried (1975), for instance, points out that studies on treated populations sometimes suggest a positive relationship between social status and "mild" disorders such as the neuroses, while field studies which measure primarily neurotic symptomatology often reveal a negative relationship. The interpretation of the Langner symptoms in this chapter would lead to the conclusion that field studies and clinical studies are not simply measuring different symptomatology and that the inconsistency in this finding needs to be examined more carefully. Clearly, the use of treated populations confounds symptomatology with help-seeking processes, as well as social factors which determine continuance in treatment. These facts taken together suggest that field studies that use symptom scales like the Langner Index should be given more weight.

It is undeniably the case that studies of psychiatric disorder should and will move toward greater use of diagnostically specific instruments such as the SADS, and will sample both treated and untreated populations for comparisons, but it is also true that the great wealth of empirical evidence that has accumulated using psychiatric symptom scales in community studies should not be ignored in assessing what we now know about psychiatric disorder.

Acknowledgments

I am indebted to Jerome K. Myers for his permission to use the 1975 data from the New Haven community survey. This research was supported by grant MH-28274 from the Alcohol, Drug Abuse, and

Mental Health Administration of the Center for Epidemiologic Studies, National Institute of Mental Health. I am also indebted to Richard L. Hough and Dianne Timbers Fairbank for providing their data from research supported by grant MH-16108 of the Center for Epidemiologic Studies, National Institute of Mental Health.

References

Carr, L.G., and N. Krause. (1978) "Social status, psychiatric symptomatology, and response bias." *J. Hlth. Soc. Behav.*, 19:86–91.

Clancy, K. & Gove, W. (1975), Sex differences in mental illness: an analysis of response bias in self-reports. *Amer. J. Sociol.*, 80:205–216.

Coleman, J.C. (1964), *Abnormal Psychology and Modern Life*. Glenview, Ill.: Scott, Foresman.

Crandell, D.L. & Dohrenwend, B.P. (1967), Some relations among psychiatric symptoms, organic illness, and social class. *Amer. J. Psychiat.*, 126:1527–1537.

Cronbach, L.J. & Meehl, P.E. (1955), Construct validy in psychological tests. *Psychol. Bull.*, 52:281–302.

Dohrenwend, B.P. & Crandell, D.L. (1970), Psychiatric symptoms in community, clinic, and mental hospital groups. *Amer. J. Psychiat.*, 126:1611–1621.

Dohrenwend, B.P. & Dohrenwend, B.S. (1969), *Social Status and Psychological Disorder*. New York: Wiley.

Eaton, W.W. (1978), Life events, social supports, and psychiatric symptoms: a re-analysis of the New Haven data. *J. Hlth Soc. Behav.*, 19:230–234.

Endicott, J. & Spitzer, R.L. (1977), A diagnostic interview: the schedule of affective disorder and schizophrenia. Read at the 130th Annual Meeting of the American Psychiatric Association, Toronto.

Fried, M. (1975), Social differences in mental health. In: *Poverty and Health: A Sociological Analysis*. rev. ed., ed. J. Kosa & I.K. Zola. Cambridge, Mass.: Harvard University Press, pp. 135–192.

Greenley, J.R. & Mechanic, D. (1976), Social selection in seeking help for psychological problems. *J. Hlth Soc. Behav.*, 17:249–262.

Haberman, P.W. (1965), An analysis of retest scores for an index of psychophysiological disturbance. *J. Hlth Hum. Behav.*, 6:257–260.

Jöreskog, K.G. (1973), A general method of estimating a linear structural equation system. In: *Structural Equation Models in the Social Sciences*, ed. A.S. Goldberger and O.D. Duncan. New York: Seminar Press, pp. 85–112.

Jöreskog, K.G. (1976), Structural equation models in the social sciences: specification, estimation, and testing. Department of Statistics, University Of Uppsala. Invited paper for the Symposium on Applications of Statistics, Dayton, Ohio.

Jöreskog, K.G. & Sörbom, D. (1977), Statistical models and methods for the analysis of longitudinal data. In: *Latent Variables in Socioeconomic Models*, ed. D.J. Aigner & A.S. Goldberger. New York: Elsevier/North Holland, 1977, pp. 285–325.

Langner, T.S. (1962), A twenty-two item screening score of psychiatric symptoms indicating impairment. *J. Hlth Hum. Behav.*, 3:269–276.

Manis, J.G., Brawer, M.J., Hunt, C.L., & Kercher, L.C. (1963), Validating a mental health scale. *Amer. Sociol. Rev.*, 28:108–116.

Micklin, M. & Leon, C.A. (1978), Life change and psychiatric disturbance in a South

American city: the effects of geographic and social mobility. *J. Hlth Soc. Behav.*, 19:92–107.

Mueller, D.P., Edwards, D.W., & Yarvis, R.M. (1977), Stressful life events and psychiatric symptomatology: change or undesirability? *J. Hlth Soc. Behav.*, 18:307–317.

Phillips, D.L. & Clancy, K.J. (1970), Response biases in field studies of mental illness. *Amer. Sociol. Rev.*, 35:403–515.

Phillips, D.L. & Segal, B.E. (1969), Sexual status and psychiatric symptoms. *Amer. Sociol. Rev.*, 34:58–72.

Schwab, J.J., McGinnis, N.H., & Warheit, G.J. (1970), Toward a social psychiatric definition of impairment. *Brit. J. Soc. Psychiat.*, 4:51–61.

Seiler, L.H. (1973), The 22-item scale used in field studies of mental illness: a question of method, a question of substance, and a question of theory. *J. Hlth Soc. Behav.*, 14:252–264.

Shader, R.I., Ebert, N.H., & Harmatz, J.S. (1971), Langner's psychiatric impairment scale: a short screening device. *Amer. J. Psychiat.*, 128:596–600.

Singer, E., Cohen, S.M., Garfinkel, R., & Srole, L. (1976), Replicating psychiatric ratings through multiple regression analysis: the midtown Manhattan restudy. *J. Hlth Soc. Behav.*, 17:376–387.

Spitzer, R.L., Endicott, J., & Robins, E. (1977), Research Diagnostic Criteria: rationale and reliability. Read at the 130th Annual Meeting of the American Psychiatric Association, Toronto.

Summers, G.F., Seiler, L.H., & Hough, R.L. (1969), Psychiatric symptoms and the use of mental health services. Project working paper No. 9, Rural Industrial Development Project, University of Illinois, Urbana, Illinois.

Tessler, R., Mechanic, D., & Dimond, M. (1976), The effect of psychological distress on physician utilization: a prospective study. *J. Hlth Soc. Behav.*, 17:353–364.

Thoits, P. & Hannan, M. (1979), Income and psychological distress: the impact of an income-maintenance experiment. *J. Hlth Soc. Behav.*, 20:120–138.

Weissman, M.M., Myers, J.K., & Harding, P.S. (1978), Psychiatric disorders in a U.S. urban community: 1975–1976. *Amer. J. Psychiat.*, 135:459–462.

Wheaton, B. (1978), The sociogenesis of psychological disorder: reexamining the causal issues with longitudinal data. *Amer. Sociol. Rev.*, 43:383–403.

Wildman, R.C. & Johnson, D.R. (1977), Life change and Langner's 22-item mental health index: a study and partial replication. *J. Hlth Soc. Behav.*, 18:179–188.

Self-Regulation and the Mechanisms for Symptom Appraisal

HOWARD LEVENTHAL

DAVID R. NERENZ

ANDREA STRAUS

Epidemiologic data play a critical role in health planning and policy formation affecting the expenditure of millions of dollars for programs in disease prevention and treatment and for the training of health-care personnel (Dingle, 1973; Ebert, 1973; White, 1973). Mechanic and Newton (1965) argue that the similarity of mortality figures in different nations and regions requires that health planning and policy formation must rely increasingly on estimates of incidence and prevalence obtained by door-to-door surveys or tests given during patient use of screening and treatment services. As is the case with any data, however, true population values for incidence and prevalence are but dimly perceived through curtains of error or noise.

The noise affecting our sample statistics can be divided into two broad classes: random and systematic. Random noise includes known contributors to sampling error. It is distressing, but can be compensated for by increasing both sample size and the reliability of measuring instruments. Systematic bias poses a far more serious problem. Increases in sample size or instrument reliability simply shrink the margin of error for estimates of a population value and increase certainty in biased values. We believe that morbidity statistics, whether based on subjective reports in door-to-door surveys or objective reports of screening and diagnostic procedures on treated patients, are biased by the psychological processes involved in the layperson's understanding of the illness experience. This chapter focuses on the psychological processes affecting awareness, reporting, and action with respect to specific symptoms, and the manner in which these processes can influence epidemiologic data. Our purpose is to present an initial picture of the information processing mechanisms involved in the way people perceive and respond to bodily complaints. We will sketch the basic features of the mental apparatus for perceiving and coping with illness symptoms. Then we will elaborate on how the mental apparatus processes information related to health and illness. Finally we will consider briefly the implications of our discussion for health planning and public policy.

The Mental Apparatus Underlying Symptom-related Behavior

When individuals notice a body sensation or a change in mood or behavior (Robinson, 1971) they may believe it represents some malfunction or illness. These events are observed and interpreted by comparing them with one's personal history and other people's past experience. From a series of such events, an individual constructs a representation of an illness episode or problem and then creates a coping plan which may or may not include formal medical treatment. This illness representation reflects the operation of an underlying information-processing mechanism, designed to regulate the individual's relationship to environmental events. Thus, its purpose is to utilize information and feedback for self-regulation (Leventhal, 1970; Leventhal et al., 1980b; Schwartz, 1979). This process is recurrent, each illness episode having a beginning point and providing a succession of informational inputs from the body or outer environment. As these inputs stimulate additional processing cycles, the episode takes on structure or form. It is perceived as a specific illness demanding particular treatments.

Features of the System—The information-processing mechanism has several characteristics that influence the way in which it deals with illness episodes.

1. Stages in processing. Information-processing systems are a series of *stages* that represent relatively discrete operations involved in the processing of new information. The system has three basic stages: (*a*) a stage of interpretation where information is analyzed and given meaning; (*b*) a stage of action-planning or coping where appropriate responses to stimuli are generated and executed; and (*c*) an appraisal stage where the results of the action stage are assessed in relation to some desired outcome. (see fig. 1). The stages are important both theoretically and practically because different kinds of information and preparation affect each of them.
2. Parallel construction. The information-processing system and the physical apparatus underlying it process information

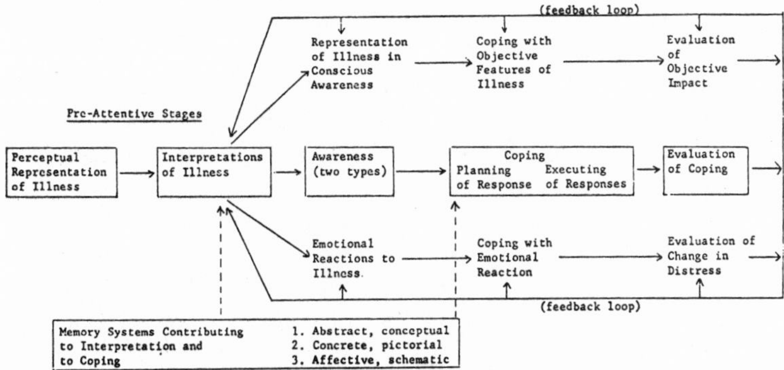

Figure 1: The Self-Regulation Processing System

through parallel routes. A major theme in our own work has been the concept of parallel routes for the subjective and objective processing of events. Objective perceptions and interpretations are distinct from the private reactions and evaluations of subjective emotional processing, and can therefore be split off from them (Leventhal, 1970, 1974). The degree to which these two routes are integrated significantly alters reactions to threat.

3. Hierarchical processing. Another important feature common to many information-processing models is that stimulus inputs are enriched or progressively more deeply processed by hierarchical levels of the nervous system. At the simplest level of processing are various automatic mechanisms which make use of very concrete stimulus features. At an intermediate level are the somewhat more abstract, flexible processes involved in perceptual memory [e.g., the ability to recognize events, locate objects, and store images of specific situations and episodes (Posner, 1973)]. Conceptual processes form a still more abstract level of information storage and processing represented in humans by the use of language. The conceptual system offers a highly flexible medium for rearranging information, appraising environments and people, and anticipating the outcome of future actions. While each level of activity can be thought of as separate and unique, in any given situation the levels operate jointly (Leventhal, 1979). It is also likely that more abstract representations are based to some degree on concrete ones, so that a noun such as chair has a more concrete denotative reference in multiple images of specific chairs (Macnamara, 1972).

4. Deliberate versus automatic processing. Much information processing occurs rapidly and automatically without conscious attention to or awareness of the processes underlying experience and behavior (Kimble and Perlmutter, 1970; Leventhal, 1974, 1980; Shiffrin and Schneider, 1977). This is especially true of the more concrete levels of perception and emotion as well as some aspects of coping. Automatic planning and coping is often a product of overlearning, such as reaching for a glass of milk when feeling dyspeptic or touching a sore area on the neck to see if it is swollen. New behaviors can be performed automatically, however, by inserting them within ongoing automatic action sequences. For example, by arranging to have lunch near a blood pressure screening site one will be prompted by external cues to have one's pressure taken without having to deliberately think about doing it (Leventhal, 1970). Emotional reactions are likely to provoke automatic (nonconsciously controlled) behavior sequences, whereas long-term planning and coping will more probably involve complex sequences of conscious imagery and thought typical of volitional or deliberate action. Behavior at any point in time, however, is likely to reflect both automatic and volitional processes.

Processing over Time— We have suggested elsewhere that the processing system is best viewed as a feedback loop in which goals for action are set, with the system operating over time until the goals are reached (Miller et al., 1960; Lazarus, 1966; Powers, 1973; Leventhal, 1970, 1980; Carver, 1979; Leventhal et al., 1980b). Perceptions, interpretations, plans, coping reactions, and evaluations all occur over time. Three principles play important roles in the ontogeny of regulatory systems:

1. The characteristics of the processing system change over time. This notion asserts that the processing system becomes more complex both within and across illness episodes. Interpretations are added, situations are differentiated, and emotions are combined to generate new feelings and skills.
2. Changes in the processing system involve both the accumulation of interpretations and coping responses specific to situations and generalized cognitive sets which are applied to a variety of problems (Harlow, 1959). Generalized sets are important to insure the transfer of interpretations and skills from earlier problem-solving situations to later ones which are similar, yet in some way different, from those already faced.

3. Temporal projections are built into perception and cognition. The representations of an illness and coping plans that make up illness cognitions will also have built-in time lines. Perceiving illness as acute rather than chronic implies brief versus long-lasting episodes, and representations of coping as effective or ineffective implies rapid versus extended recovery times.

Stability and Instability of Self-Regulatory Systems—When the output of perception, interpretation, and coping meets specified goals and the regulatory system stabilizes, the behaviors associated with it become automatic and less demanding of conscious attention. An effective system will function as a negative feedback unit (von Bertalanffy, 1968; Schwartz, 1979) and facilitate adaptive activity at low to moderately high levels of arousal. If the output of the system does *not* meet expectations, if, for instance, treatment increases rather than decreases symptoms and distress, there is an increase in arousal and a deployment of more conscious attention and effort to the behaviors and their goals. Schwartz (1979) coined the term "disregulation" to define breakdowns in regulatory processes, and he identified the failure to monitor critical cues and attend to them as a major source of disregulation.

The Information-processing System and Epidemiology

To describe the manner in which psychological processes affect epidemiologic data, we will consider how an information-processing mechanism might operate and affect each stage in the development of an illness episode. These stages include: generating and noticing symptoms; appraising the symptom to determine its causes and consequences; coping with the symptom if such efforts seem necessary; integrating information from practitioners; and assessing the effectiveness of coping efforts.

Generating and Noticing Symptoms: Why People Feel Bad—Zola (1973) suggests that a naive extrapolation from the medical model leads to the expectation that diagnosed illness directly reflects incidence and prevalence of illness in a community. In this model, an illness agent affects physiological processes producing a disease and symptoms, and symptoms lead directly to help seeking. But there is no direct link between illness, symptoms and symptom reports, and the use of the medical care system (Mechanic, 1963; Suchman, 1965; Zola, 1973; Safer et al., 1979). What are the sources of bodily symptoms? It is obvious that disease agents create physical and physiological upset and make a major contribution to symptom states. However, the biological being has ways of minimizing the impact of disease agents (Antonovsky, 1979). The degree to which we interpret events as challenges or threats and see life as meaningful and coherent or vacuous and disorganized appears to play an important role in resistance to pervasive agents (Kobasa, 1979; Antonovsky, 1979). Unstable solutions to environmental threats appear to generate directly emotional reactions and psychological distress accompanied by an array of psychophysiological symptoms. Thus, symptoms can be generated by disease agents, by the psychophysiological correlates of stability or instability in the information-processing system, and by such interactions of the two as the effects of processing on susceptibility to disease agents.

Perhaps the most obvious impact of the above processes on epidemiologic data is their effect on symptom perception and reporting, which will be most noticeable in the diagnosis of specific illnesses via survey methods and estimates of prevalence and incidence. We will discuss three specific ways in which these influences are felt.

Disregulation of the hierarchical system—When coping proceeds successfully, our automatic response mechanisms, perceptual images, and conceptualizations lead to similar representations and ways of coping with situations. Disregulations typically reflect inconsistencies in the system accompanied by breakdowns in automatic reactions, the inhibition of ongoing action, and increased attention and effort directed at previously unnoticed features of the setting (Dewey, 1894; Mandler and Watson, 1966; Schwartz, 1979; Leventhal and Nerenz, 1980). In feedback theory these are situations where the coping process generates positive feedback and increases organismic arousal. All of this makes heavy demands on coping capabilities.

Breakdowns in regulation and excessive demands on the regulatory system are major determinants of seeking medical care (Zola, 1973) and are heavily implicated in the onset of illness (Rahe, 1972a, 1972b). Recent reports implicate life events in susceptibility to acute infectious disease (Mason et al., 1979; Gruchow, 1979). Disregulation of social relationships (e.g., loss of a spouse), plays a critical role in the onset and recovery from depression (Brown et al., 1973).

A more direct indication that disregulation itself can generate symptomatology is provided by Pennebaker et al. (1977). Their subjects were able to terminate a 95-decibel noise by pushing a button. In one group of subjects the noise stopped after every five button presses; in a second group the noise stopped after an average of five button presses, with the actual number of presses varying from trial to trial. The subjects who pressed five times every trial felt more in control of the stressor since they could perform five button presses and regulate their exposure to the noise rapidly and with little attention or effort. The subjects working on the random schedule could never be sure when they would or would not succeed in turning off the noxious stimulus. Questionnaire data showed that the latter subjects felt less control over the noxious stimulus. After they left the experiment all subjects were stopped in the hall and asked by another investigator to complete a 59-item questionnaire which included 13 questions on symptoms. The results showed that subjects who had been exposed to the random schedule reported significantly more symptomatology in areas such as heart racing, shortness of breath, itching, flushed face, and dizziness. Thus, the data strongly suggest that states of disregulation can generate symptomatology.

Emotions and symptoms—Combining a body sensation with an emotional interpretation, and thus coding the sensation in a concrete memory of pain and distress (Leventhal and Everhart, 1979) appears to have at least three consequences. First, the arousal of subjective emotion and its visceral autonomic components appears to intensify body sensations such as pain and distress. This is seen in the above study by Pennebaker et al. (1977), in Beecher's (1946) field observations of pain and distress in men wounded in combat, and pain and distress experienced during childbirth (Javert and Hardy, 1950; Leventhal and Sharpe, 1965) and surgery (Janis, 1958; Johnson et al., 1971, 1978). Second, emotion can generate a wide range of psychophysiological sensations to which are added other nonillness sensations, creating a more diffuse sensory representation. This is seen in the different symptom presentations of ethnic groups. Italian and Jewish patients show emotional involvement and present symptoms in a general and diffuse manner, while Irish patients focus on a precise set of sensations that are most related to their illness (Zborowski, 1969; Zola, 1973).

The third consequence of combining emotion with body sensations is the possibility of storing vivid memories of the experienced pain and distress and reactivating these memories under times of emotional stress. For example, emotional arousal appears to facilitate the development of a phantom limb, which is the experience of the presence of a painful limb following its amputation (Simmel, 1962; Melzack, 1971). This is not a memory about pain, but the reactivation of a pain experience. The arousal of emotion due to stressful life events appears to reactivate phantom pain experiences after these phantom pains had faded away (Melzack, 1973).

Disease labels and symptoms—Being told one has an illness also appears to generate symptomatology. Our own studies indicate that people search for physical symptoms to make sense of illness labels.

For example, simply being told that one has a high blood pressure reading directs attention to the body and initiates a symptom search process (Meyer et al., 1980). The search, however, is not undirected. The meaning of hypertension and cultural notions about hypertension focus the individual on specific cues. This was evident in comparisons made between six groups of respondents: hypertensives newly discovered at a screening site (n = 50), hypertensives newly treated under professional care (n = 65), hypertensives in continuing treatment 6 months to 30-plus years (n = 52), and hypertensives reentering treatment, having previously dropped out (n = 65). Nearly all (>90%) of the continuing treatment and reentry patients believed they had a symptom of hypertension by which they could tell when their blood pressure was elevated. They monitored headaches, dizziness, facial flushing, feelings of tension, and so forth. Only 71% of the newly treated patients engaged in symptom monitoring, but this figure changed to over 90% 6 months after their first treatment visit. Thus, increasing numbers of people develop symptomatic representations of their illness as treatment progresses. The symptoms reported also change over time. Newly discovered and newly treated hypertensives are likely to attend to heartbeats because they associate stress and cardiac activity with high blood pressure, while none of the continuing treatment or reentry patients monitor heartbeats as a sign of high blood pressure.

It is interesting to observe people at a screening site when they are told they have high blood pressure. Those accompanied by friends may be teased about being uptight and tense—this belief that stress causes high blood pressure is clearly articulated. Among people with newly discovered elevations in pressure, 45% regard stress as a determinant of their problem. It should come as no surprise that they notice their heart beating when told their pressure is elevated, since this information probably makes them tense and nervous. This bodily activity can, in turn, automatically bring to mind other occasions when they were anxious and tense and had a noticeable heartbeat. The emotion activates memories of past episodes of this sort, thus creating the intuitive conviction that stress is indeed the determinant of their hypertension.

The need to relate concrete symptoms and abstract disease concepts can produce much bias in symptom report data. Awareness of illness in others may, for example, heighten sensitivity to body changes, leading to exaggerated reports of illness (false positives). Indeed, there is even a possibility of symptom contagion. Observing symptoms in others or hearing disease labels applied to others could focus attention on similar symptoms in oneself and even activate prototypic perceptual memories of past illness experiences that would generate symptom experiences. Medical students' disease appears to be a prime example of this phenomenon (Woods et al., 1966).

Objective medical tests on people who come for treatment do not circumvent the biases introduced by patients' generation of symptoms. For instance, Mechanic has discussed social and cultural influences that can bring people into the medical care system and generate greater use of screening and primary care services (Mechanic, 1972). This could also result in the detection in these groups of a higher proportion of individuals with chronic illness; infrequent users of the medical care system might die of other ills while their chronic illnesses go undiscovered. Whether the initial symptomatology of an illness is severe, mild, or moderate could also affect our knowledge of its natural history and have substantial impact on the development of complex cultural models of causation and illness experience. One might speculate that the apparently greater fear associated with cancer in contrast to heart disease is related to the uncertainty associated with the long-term nature and unclear onset of the former. These emotional reactions may be responsible for strenuous efforts at early detection by some people while others delay in response to relatively severe symptoms.

Expectations and symptoms—In situations where illnesses occur on a regular or cyclic basis, people seem to generate symptoms simply because they expect the symptoms to occur. Tax accountants who view stress as a cause of cardiac disease may think their heart problems recur each year in early April (Friedman et al., 1957).

Women who associate being ill with the menstrual cycle expect it to occur on a monthly basis. Ruble and Brooks-Gunn (1979) have argued that the occurrence of menstrual symptoms each month is largely generated by temporal expectations. Given a history of occasional physiological upset with menses and a clearly cyclical representation of menstruation, it is possible that the conceptualization recruits concrete perceptual memories of symptomatology so that physiological distress is actually experienced at this time. Ruble

(1977) tested this hypothesis by randomly assigning a sample of women to two conditions: one in which they were told tests indicated their menstrual period was due immediately; another in which they were told it was due in a week to ten days. The first group of women experienced considerably more "menstrual" symptoms during the week following the communication, although the actual onset of menstruation for both groups of women was about a week away. Thus, expectations about onset generated cognitive changes that were associated with menstrual symptomatology.

It is not known how many illnesses are perceived to be associated with cycles such as this. At least one woman in Meyer's (1980) sample associated high blood pressure with her menstrual period. She made the association because she was edematous at that time and knew her blood pressure medication removed water from the body. She altered her medication to correspond to this cycle, taking more medication during the menses and skipping it during the intervening period.

Two compensating sources of epidemiologic bias are present here. On the one hand, the association between regular events and illness may be overestimated since symptoms are based on expectations rather than real pathology. On the other hand, a new illness which occurs at, say, the beginning of a menstrual cycle may be attributed to the menses and not given full attention.

Symptom Appraisal: How People Decide They Are Ill

Each illness episode has its own developmental history. Safer et al. (1979) have defined three stages of development. The appraisal period lasts from the first awareness of a body change to the decision that one is ill, typically including an information search. Then comes an illness period of waiting, self-examination, and discussion with others which ends with the decision to seek professional medical help. The utilization period encompasses the time elapsed between this decision and one's actual entry into the health care system. The ontogeny of illness episodes need not be uniform (Fabrega, 1973, 1975). An episode may begin with external rather than internal information as in the case of hypertension or many cancers where the practitioner's diagnosis is the first sign of illness. Regardless of the exact pattern of the illness episode, however, there is a stage in which symptoms are appraised, or given a disease label.

Research on symptoms and illness illustrates the importance of the labeling process. When people notice unexplained or unexpected bodily signs, they search for information to interpret them

(Suchman, 1965; Robinson, 1971; Mechanic, 1972; Leventhal, 1975). This may involve talking to other people to find out if they have similar symptoms or were exposed to similar events. Social comparison processes of this sort typically are reported early in the process of symptom awareness (Safer et al., 1979).

Some conditions seem to strongly encourage information search while others appear to interfere with or short-circuit this process. If a symptom is severe or unusual, such as intense pain or profuse bleeding, there will be strong motivation to seek medical assistance for relief of pain, repair of damage, and protection against death, and the information search process will be short-circuited (Suchman, 1965; Safer et al., 1979). Severe pain demands relief.

The need for information and the tendency to seek labels is also greatly reduced if the symptoms fit what we earlier defined as a perceptual memory. For example, a substantial proportion of patients with cardiovascular disease delay in discussing their symptoms with other people and neglect (perhaps fatally) to seek treatment because they interpret their symptoms as signs of gastrointenstinal upset (Hackett and Cassem, 1969) or some other nonthreatening disease (Simon et al., 1972). Mechanic (1972) gives examples of adjustment to long-lasting symptoms which he calls normalization. People may become accustomed to symptoms such as large tumors or regard them as safe and part of ordinary bodily processes if the symptom is relatively stable over long periods of time.

On the other hand, the symptoms may be novel and different from prior illness representations. This condition encourages the seeking of professional help. It seems likely, therefore, that survey data will underestimate the prevalence of chronic and highly familiar symptoms and overestimate the prevalence of novel and unusual symptoms. Careful wording of questions could overcome this problem to some degree.

Coping: Why People Seek Medical Care

We have already mentioned that unusual and severe symptoms short-circuit the appraisal process and bring patients quickly to medical care settings. Two sets of factors affect both the decision to seek care and the type of care sought and obtained from the practitioner. The first set focuses on whether a symptom is interpreted according to emotional or objective memory codes, the second on the relationship between the cognitive representation and the coping plans of an illness.

The effect on coping of emotional and objective interpretations—When bodily sensations or symptoms are interpreted as threats and provoke subjective feelings of fear, disgust, or helplessness, they are subjectively processed. When they are processed as events, i.e., the way a physician or nurse might regard them in another person, they are objectively processed. Although the two types of processing occur simultaneously, they affect behavior differently. For example, when we compare reactions to high and low fear warnings to take tetanus innoculations or reduce weight and stop smoking, we usually find more negative attitudes toward the threat and stronger intentions to act following the high rather than following the low fear message (Leventhal et al., 1965, 1966, 1967).

Fear can also have negative effect. For example, when high threat messages are used to warn subjects of low self-esteem about a health danger, the fear stimulated by the threat appears to generate feelings of hopelessness about their ability to cope with the threat. For this population, a high fear message results in less of the recommended protective behavior than does a low fear message. Most of the effects of fear are short-lived, however. Within a few days, or a few weeks at most, there is no longer any advantage to the high fear message (Leventhal and Niles, 1965) and even the negative effects may fade (Kornzweig, 1967). Long term effects, such as taking tetanus shots (Leventhal et al., 1965; Kornzweig, 1967) or reducing smoking (Leventhal et al., 1967; Rogers and Mewborn, 1976) are also detectable, but these seem to depend on cognitive (rather than emotional) features of the threat information. Thus, one can detect equally strong long-term effects from weak or strong fear messages in comparison to control groups unexposed to threat information.

One important effect of emotional processing on coping is that the individual may seek care in order to control his or her emotions rather than to receive treatment for the underlying physical disorder or the situational events stimulating either the symptom or the emotion. Shuval (1970) has documented the way utilization of the health care system eases the distress generated from recent immigration and the difficulty of adapting to a new culture. Repetitive use of the health care system motivated by emotional needs appears to be an important factor in the labeling of patients as psychiatrically ill by primary care practitioners (Cleary, 1980). One consequence of this diagnosis is the administration of tranquilizing agents. The percentage of people labeled this way greatly exceeds the proportion of psychiatric problems that would be found by thorough psychiatric diagnoses (Rosen et al., 1972; Goldberg, 1974).

Sex differences in incidence and prevalence of illness and in the utilization of medical services provide another example of the way self-regulatory systems may influence these areas of epidemiologic and policy concern. Women live longer than men, yet report more symptoms (Phillips and Segal, 1969; Nathanson, 1975), are more sensitive to pressures that generate psychiatric illness (Gove and Tudor, 1973), and make greater use of medical services (U.S. Dept. HEW, 1973). Is there truly greater morbidity among women than men? If so, how can their greater longevity be explained? Perhaps sex differences reflect differences in the regulatory systems for interpreting and coping with body sensation. Women seem more ready to include bodily reactions in their emotional and judgmental processes (Cupchik and Leventhal, 1974; Leventhal, 1974; Svebak, 1975). Women also appear to be more open and freer in communicating personal feelings (Phillips and Segal, 1969). If women are more likely to attach emotional significance to bodily sensation and to talk about feelings and body changes, would this not account for the bulk of sex differences in the prevalence of illness and utilization of medical services? The fit between the sex difference data in health and illness behavior and the processing model proposed here further emphasizes the potential significance of processing mechanisms for a number of basic concerns in epidemiology and the delivery of health services.

The link between illness representation and coping—Prior investigations of the effects of fear-arousing communications on preventive health actions (such as quitting smoking and taking tetanus innoculations) found that information to generate action plans had no effect on emotional reactions, attitudes toward the threat, or intentions to take protective action. The action plans did produce substantial increases in taking tetanus shots and long-term compliance with anti-smoking recommendations. The information used to generate action plans included maps locating where to go for a tetanus innoculation and suggestions to review one's program so as to incorporate this behavior into ongoing activity (Leventhal et al., 1965, 1966) or instructions on how to quit smoking cigarettes, such as planning a quit day, selecting substitutes for purchase, and practicing ways of refusing cigarettes (Leventhal et al., 1967). Thus, action plans and the rehearsal of coping strategies have substantial effects on the execution of responses and little if any effects on the representation of the health threat.

Although different kinds of information affect the representation of health threat and coping, it would be wrong to conclude that there is no link between the two. Subjects given an action plan without a message about the danger do not take tetanus shots or reduce smoking. Both a representation of the threat and a representation of the coping behavior are necessary for action. The link between the representation of a health danger and coping is still closer when one examines behavior in situations of stress. For example, patients given instructions on how to cope with an endoscopy exam (how to breathe when their throats are painted with anesthetic, how to swallow the fiber optic camera tube) perform these behaviors more effectively if they also receive detailed information on body sensations and can anticipate and develop an objective or nonthreatening representation of the danger (Johnson and Leventhal, 1974). A close relationship between coping and the objective representation of a stressor was also seen in two studies of labor and delivery: women who monitored their labor contractions were better able to push during the final stage of delivery and were less angry, frightened, and tense at that time. Monitoring contractions did not benefit them at other points in the delivery. A facilitative effect of sensation information on coping was also found in a Johnson et al. (1978) study of cholecystectomy surgeries. Women given both sensation information and an action plan were discharged from hospital nearly a full day before women in the control groups and were also back on their feet and out of their homes three days earlier than controls. These field experiments emphasize the important linkage between planning and rehearsing coping behaviors and the availability of an objective representation of a stressful situation. If the stress stimulus is accurately perceived and not experienced as a threat, the individual is better able to regulate himself or herself during the stress episode. In short, behaviors can produce desired effects and generate needed feedback when they are directed by a good map of the problem environment.

The studies described above illustrate links between illness representations and coping which led to beneficial outcomes. These outcomes were beneficial because the representation of the problem provided an accurate map of underlying processes. An "objective," nonemotional representation of a problem may not reflect actual medical processes. It seems that representations of illness problems will be in error when the problem departs from the individual's past concrete experience with illness. This is most evident in chronic conditions that develop asymptomatically. People who are asymptomatic are likely to perceive themselves as well; people who are symptomatic are likely to perceive themselves as ill. Thus, when told they are ill, they expect to be symptomatic and will monitor and evaluate treatment outcomes by comparing them to a model of acute illness. Outcomes of this sort are particularly noticeable in our studies of hypertensives (Meyer et al., 1980).

Regardless of their "accuracy," illness representations and coping strategies can interact with disease processes in ways that are subtle, but have a major impact on epidemiologic statistics. Let us take, for example, the problem of estimating the prevalence of different cancers from screening programs. The data on different types of cancer will reflect their actual prevalence in the population. But screening results are also affected by the duration of the presymptomatic phase. Cancers that develop slowly will appear to be more prevalent than rapidly developing cancers because people with the latter type of disease are more likely to be in treatment and so not go for screening. If the population available for screening is well informed and believes the disease can be detected and treated, large numbers will appear for screening and more disease will be detected for the cancer with the longer preclinical period.

A quite different epidemiologic and treatment situation will hold if the population believes disease is symptomatic. In this instance, diseases with lengthy preclinical phases are likely to be underdetected in comparison to those that develop rapidly. If the disease process is reversible only in the early preclinical phase, the belief that disease must be symptomatic will reduce the likelihood of favorable treatment outcomes. The accumulation of such negative experiences could reinforce population perceptions of the disease as hopeless and stimulate further delays in screening, thus decreasing treatability.

The interactions between preventive health behaviors and illness processes can become yet more complex. Continuing with the above example, assume that a new screening device is developed and subjected to field testing. If the test population is protectively oriented and has been repeatedly screened, those people with relatively advanced preclinical cases of the cancer will have been removed, and the sensitivity of the screening test would be underestimated. Furthermore, one might conclude that the subsequent treatment is extending life spans when it has merely detected the disease in an earlier part of the preclinical phase—an issue of lead-time bias (Cole and Morrison, 1978).

Knowledge about the natural history of a disease and the screening experience and health beliefs of the target population are as critical for the evaluation of prevalence as is an understanding of the screening device.

Evaluation: Why People Remain in Treatment

The use of symptoms—When we examine factors that lead patients either to remain in treatment or drop out of the medical care system, the determinant of primary importance seems to be how the patients' symptoms change as a result of treatment. Patients rely on concrete indicators such as symptoms to tell them when treatment is effective, and patients often drop out if a treatment (even a successful one) does not have a measurable impact on such indicators.

Meyer's study of patient compliance with antihypertension medication illustrates this point (Meyer et al., 1980). His patients in continuing treatment showed a high level of conceptual knowledge about their illness and treatment but a relatively low level of compliance: 88% knew the names of their medications, 94% knew the prescribed schedule, 92% could list two or more risks, but only 35% reported strict adherence to treatment regimens. Paradoxically, while 80% of these patients agreed that hypertension was asymptomatic, 88% were quite sure they could use symptoms to detect elevations in their *own* blood pressure. More importantly, the patient's perception that treatment affected his or her symptoms was related to compliance and blood pressure control: 61% (11/18) of these patients with borderline or poor control of blood pressure saw no effect of treatment on their symptomatology, while 83% (15/18) of well-controlled patients believed their treatment alleviated their symptoms. An examination of the reentry patients showed that 34% had dropped out because treatment did not improve their symptom state and 32% had dropped out when their synptoms failed to return after they ran out of medication. Many of these patients reentered treatment because the reappearance of a familiar symptom led them to seek screening and they once again registered a high reading. A high proportion of these patients (80%) dropped out of treatment a second time; the disappearance of the symptoms again persuaded them that the illness was in remission. They acted as though they expected the disease to cycle. By contrast, patients who returned to treatment with a new symptom behaved quite differently; only 13% of these patients dropped out of treatment. These patients may place greater reliance on the physician's reports of blood pressure levels because the variation in their symptoms made them uncertain of their ability to monitor changes in their illness.

These findings illustrate the way concrete symptoms control coping and how clarity of feedback from coping can affect the individual's conception of the state of his or her illness. Why do concrete signs play so critical a role in determining the relationship between the representation of an illness and coping? This is a crucial question because Meyer found no relationship between blood pressure levels and symptoms in his sample. The answer to this question is relatively simple. By monitoring symptoms patients can appraise the current state of their illness. They can tell if the condition is getting better, worse, or remaining unchanged and so know if the treatment is working. An effective treatment should reduce or eliminate the symptom, while an ineffective one will leave the symptom unchanged. A dangerous treatment will exacerbate the symptom and may add unpleasant symptoms of its own. In addition, the individual can use the symptom to mark the onset of the disease and isolate the conditions which provoked it. For example, a hypertensive individual may recall similar symptoms of heart racing, headache, and dizziness during times of stress which would help identify the onset of the hypertensive disorder and pinpoint specific environmental events (e.g., job stress or family conflict) as causes of hypertension.

There seem to be at least three different reasons why symptoms play so important a role in linking illness representations and coping for chronic conditions. First, because the condition lasts over a long period of time, the symptom provides the only continual and readily available information for monitoring and appraising the impact of environmental events and practitioner's and self-prescribed treatments on the underlying condition. Symptoms are readily available. Second, it seems that people treat symptoms as highly valid indicators of illness. They act as though the body does not lie. Third, symptom appraisal can take place with little attention and effort. The ease of such automatic behaviors makes them efficient ways of determining one's illness status.

The significance of the symptom in linking the representation of illness to coping is illustrated by the examples already given and by other data suggesting how much difficulty patients have when they are asymptomatic. For example, lymphoma patients whose symptoms remit abruptly with treatment are much more distressed during chemotherapy than patients whose symptoms show more gradual remission (Nerenz, 1979). The abrupt remission deprives patients of clear information about the state of their condition and makes it difficult for them to justify the continuation of a distressing treatment. A similar effect has been found in an unpublished report by Gutmann (1980): coronary bypass patients who were asymptomatic prior to surgery did very well during and immediately after surgery, but weeks later began to show signs of distress because they had no clear way of evaluating whether their condition had worsened or improved. They were uncertain about the outcome of surgery, since they had no reason to believe their body could provide them with direct and rapid feedback about the state of their heart.

These data indicate that patients' presence in treatment settings and appearance in epidemiologic statistics will depend on the extent to which treatments have a visible impact on illness symptoms. The success rate of certain treatments may also be underestimated if the treatment affects the underlying agent but does not immediately change the appearance of symptoms. Diseases that are initially asymptomatic are especially likely to be affected by these biases since treatment will either have no impact on symptoms or introduce symptoms of its own. In either case, patients are likely to drop out of the medical care system and be left out of prevalence and incidence estimates.

Assessment Strategies—There are particular ways in which symptoms are used to decide whether an illness is getting better or worse, how accurate one's diagnosis is, and what the response to treatment is. Two strategies that can be applied to resolving these time-ordered questions are (*a*) the contingency rule and (*b*) the similarity rule.

The temporal contingency between changes in bodily sensations and outside events plays a critical role in interpreting an illness episode and in differentiating experiences of treatment from those caused by the illness itself. Since treatment is usually a salient experience, we can expect it to orient the individual to his or her body. The temporal relationships between treatment and symptoms play a major role in differentiating illness and treatment representations and in evaluating treatment in cancer chemotherapy (Nerenz, 1979; Ringler, 1980). Chemotherapy produces a wide range of physical symptoms including nausea, hair loss, tiredness, and loss of appetite. Because most of these symptoms follow treatment in an orderly, time-contingent manner, they are generally attributed to the chemotherapy rather than the illness. Even when symptoms do not directly follow treatment, specific information about contingencies aids in the attribution process. Thus, in contrast to nausea which begins an hour or two after an injection, hair loss can occur at any time during a four-week "cycle" of chemotherapy. Preparation by the practitioners readies the patient for the experience of hair loss and assists him or her in integrating it with the treatment rather than incorporating it with the illness and interpreting the hair loss as a sign of the exacerbation of disease and decomposition of his or her body.

The similarity of a current bodily sensation to an earlier symptom pattern is a second factor that plays an important role in the interpretation of and response to current symptoms. Individuals seem to expect more intense versions of a specific set of symptoms as an illness becomes more severe and less intense symptoms as the illness becomes better; they do not seem to expect marked changes in the symptoms' structural characteristics (location and sensory qualities). We have previously described how many patients confuse cardiovascular disease symptoms with gastrointestinal distress (Hackett and Cassem, 1975). One reason for the confusion in patients with *prior* coronary disease is that the current symptom experience may fail to repeat the symptoms of the initial illness episode (Hackett and Cassem, 1969). The fear aroused on earlier occasions may stimulate close attention to the symptom pattern, and the mental rehearsal of this pattern would develop a clear picture of the structural properties of the symptoms. Since current symptoms are seldom identical to those of an initial experience, the patient may assume that the new symptoms are related to some other disorder.

Gutmann (1980) reports this operation of the similarity heuristic in her study of coronary bypass patients. In this instance, patients confuse postoperative symptoms with the symptoms generated by preoperative illness. This experience is extremely threatening because it implies that the operation failed to achieve a cure. Patients with malignant lymphoma and breast cancer also identify recurrences on the basis of similarity rules, and so look for tumors primarily in places where previous tumors had disappeared rather than at new sites.

The tendency of patients to look for similar symptoms as signs of recurrence, combined with the ability of patients to generate symptoms on the basis of expectations, may produce a bias toward higher reporting of disease recurrence in door-to-door surveys. On the other hand, recurrences characterized by symptoms different from those that accompanied the initial illness will be underestimated in both surveys and patient counts since patients will often not see the new symptoms as signs of illness.

Temporal Expectations—Patients' expectations about symptoms experience are part of a larger set of expectations held about illness. Some of our recent research suggests that expectations about symptoms reflect basic time-ordered scripts or schemata that may underlie all illness-treatment cognition. Meyer (1980) has suggested that three schemata underlie specific treatment episodes for hypertension: (1) acute, (2) cyclic, and (3) chronic. These schemata appear to be conceptual representations abstracted from observations of repeated illness episodes.

The acute illness schema is probably the most important conceptual script underlying the processing of symptom and verbal information about illness. This script is a commonsense abstraction of everyday illness experiences, what Engel (1977) refers to as biomedical dogma. The acute schema treats disease as a discrete, concrete entity with specific causal agents, symptoms, breakdowns in physiological process, and curative interventions. [See Thomas (1977) for an example of this type of thought in a discussion of prevention.] This schematic view tends to focus the individual on one single cause of a disease rather than on multiple complex interactions and leads him or her to expect specific symptoms as signs of specific diseases. Medical interventions are expected to cure without any active participation on the patient's part other than "taking one's medicine." Approximately 30% of Meyer's (1980) hypertensives held an acute model of their disorder; they expect that their pressure will drop with medication and that they will stop treatment when it returns to normal and will be cured. Similarly, Ringler (1980) found that many women with breast cancer had difficulty accepting the distress of chemotherapy because they thought surgery had cured their cancer (the lump and agent were gone). Gutmann (1980) found that coronary bypass patients felt they had been cured if they no longer experienced angina and/or other cardiovascular symptoms postsurgically. It appears likely that the vast majority of illness episodes are organized in terms of an acute model and that this model affects expectations about and use of medical services.

The cyclic schema is a concatenation of acute illness models. The individual expects treatment to produce cure, but the cure is temporary and recurrence likely. The repetition may take place because of reinfection, periodic changes in susceptibility (e.g., loss of strength due to aging or fatigue), or other factors, including "fate." The perceived cause of the cycle is likely to be a significant determinant of the expected periodicity of illness.

The chronic model implies acceptance of the illness process as permanent. Chronic illness schemata appear to differ from the other schemata in a number of ways, the most important of which seems to be the degree to which the illness is seen as central to the self. If the illness is central to the self, so that it literally defines the individual's life, the illness role becomes coextensive with the individual's basic self-definition and she or he focuses interpersonal relationships and economic issues on the illness. Chronic pain patients provide an excellent example of this model (Sternbach, 1974; Fordyce, 1976).

Although the chronic pain patient represents one example of a chronic illness schema, there are others in which patients accept the permanent nature of the disease, yet come to terms with their illness. These individuals see their illness as something that deserves no more than the attention needed to care for it and minimize the degree to which it interferes with other ongoing life activities. They accept the disability and distress of the illness, yet do what they have to do and want to do. Sternbach (1974) describes how such patients present themselves at a pain clinic. They make clear that they would like to try a treatment and are willing to work at it, but that they are not willing to enter a treatment if it is chancy and requires giving up work or social relationships. Life comes first, illness and pain second. They can live with a disorder and are unwilling to sacrifice themselves to it.

Integrating Feedback: The Effect of Practitioner Communications

The practitioner's goal is to form a good picture of the disease process and develop an effective treatment plan, tasks which are enhanced by clear information from the patient and patient compliance with treatment recommendations (Sackett, 1976; Sackett and Haynes, 1976; Leventhal et al., 1980a). Unfortunately, inconsistent communications from practitioners and failure to monitor patient behavior may allow patients to develop incorrect representations of their illness and reinforce inappropriate and dangerous coping strategies (Svarstad, 1976). Practitioners are not the only ones to participate in maladaptive communication networks: family, friends, and media all contribute. Two examples will suffice: (1) The effects of positive instances on the development of illusory correlations between symptoms and illness; and (2) the reinforcement of chronic, maladaptive illness behavior.

Developing Illusory Correlations—The Chapmans (1969) have warned about illusory correlations between specific signs (e.g., peculiar eyes in drawn faces) and diagnostic categories (e.g., paranoia). Perfectly invalid signs are regularly used by clinical practitioners. An apparent reason for this is the high availability in memory of commonsense signs that are "validated" by occasional examples from clinical practice. Every practitioner's "clinical experience" includes some memorable instances where X was a sign of Y, and many less memorable instances where X predicted nothing and

Y was not preceded by X. Patients are no different. A well-trained masters' level nursing instructor had clear evidence of an association between headache and hypertension: whenever she had headaches of a particular type, she took her pressure, found it elevated, and treated herself with diuretics. Unfortunately, she failed to take her pressure when she was asymptomatic (Meyer, 1980). Practitioners may readily reinforce these illusions. If a patient claims headaches are a sign of high blood pressure, it is not unlikely that a practitioner will suggest taking pressures at these times. If the patient is chronically hypertensive, this will lead to an illusory correlation, since a headache will always be accompanied by high readings. The practitioner must place greater emphasis on taking pressures when asymptomatic, for positive instances stand out for both practitioner and patient.

If one hopes to find out that he or she is well, a negative test result will be a positive finding. If one is seeking to find out whether a symptom predicts illness, a positive test result will be a positive finding. Both questions can build illusory correlations that will be of concern to patient, practioner, and epidemiologist. For example, those who seek cancer screening tests to prove that they are well may develop a sense of invulnerability and fail to show reasonable vigilance if their screening test shows no sign of illness. Because a positive result is memorable, individuals may be lulled into a false sense of security. On the other hand, a patient may repeatedly enter and leave treatment on the basis of an illusory correlation between headache and hypertension. If different clinics are used, each entry may be counted as a new instance of the disorder. This behavior could inflate the perceived incidence of the disease, as well as leave the individual at risk for untreated hypertension when asymptomatic.

Reinforcing Chronic Illness Behavior—In most cases, the major goal for coping is the elimination of symptoms and disease and the return to health. In some cases, however, goals from other behavioral systems, such as needs for attention or sympathy, can override the goal of coping with illness and result in the adoption of a "sick role." When patients develop this form of behavior, their symptom experiences and emotional distress may be perpetuated by practitioners, concerned family and friends, and other patients. Sympathetic interest in the patient and his or her symptoms and distress can sustain those bodily signs through reinforcement and the activation of perceptual and emotional memories. The treatment which was formerly a consequence of illness behavior becomes its cause.

Investigators have identified specific behaviors that make up the sick role, including demands for care and attention, displays of helplessness, excessive compliance (expressions of respect and appreciation for every action of a physician), veiled hostility, threats of harm to self, threats to leave treatment if more help is not forthcoming, argumentativeness over details of treatment, dividing professional staff, and silliness (Wooley et al., 1978). These behaviors can be seen in patients presenting with a wide range of medical complaints and a variety of psychiatric diagnoses. They appear to elicit behaviors from practitioners and other patients that encourage and reinforce the illness role. Wooley and her colleagues devised a program of therapist reactions that provide no rewards for these behaviors but do reward actions that reflect increasing independence and return to normal life patterns, thus establishing new goals for action. By continually rewarding new behaviors, the practitioner can lead patients to revise their ways of perceiving, interpreting, and coping with the social environment, and so help to establish a new self-regulatory system.

Two important factors distinguish individuals whose illness is central to their self-image (the sick-role patients) from those who regard illness as a characteristic with which they must live. These are (1) the action plans and strategies used for coping with life problems, and (2) the emotional and/or affective tone of the individual's social relationships. Wooley et al. (1978) suggest that the chronically ill people who live a sick role orient all coping strategies to their disease. They limit work, play, and social activities to conform with the demands of their illness, focus conversations on the illness, evaluate others in terms of their attentive consideration to their pain needs, expect practitioners to provide relief from symptoms and cure for the underlying disease, and fail to take an active part in the treatment process. The chronic-pain literature offers many examples of patients whose lives have become focused on their pain. They do nothing other than attend to and attempt to control their pain, and subject themselves to considerable iatrogenic risk by seeking and demanding endless treatment. Thus, chronic-pain patients are typically grossly overmedicated and have been subjected to successive (unsuccessful) neurosurgical procedures for pain control. These individuals are usually depressed and distressed. They show elevated scores on the so-called neurotic triad (depression, hypochondriasis, and hysteria) of personality tests such as the MMPI, and typically exhibit dysphoric affect and express feelings of helplessness and loss of hope (Woodforde and Fielding, 1970).

The Influence of Cultural Beliefs on Illness Behavior

Patients' theories of illness are based on a variety of information sources, one of which deserves special mention here. Widely held cultural beliefs about illness and its treatment underlie the specific cognitions that can be seen in individual patients. These beliefs affect patients' behavior in all stages of the illness episode. As an example of the influence of beliefs on generation of symptoms, it is reasonably clear that cultural norms correlate the severity of symptomatology positively to the severity of life events. For example, severe or extensive injuries are expected to lead to intense pain, though the evidence suggests that surface injuries are often far more painful than the destruction of deeper tissues (Beecher, 1946; Chaves and Barber, 1975). It is likely that similar expectations hold about the links between the magnitude of a symptom or illness threat and the magnitude of life stresses. To the extent that patients share this belief, they will expect (and probably experience) a variety of symptoms following a stressful event (Marlatt, 1976). The belief that a serious disease will necessarily produce severe pain and must be the result of an equally severe antecedent may also play an important part in the causal analysis of heart disease or cancer. Their seriousness and threat to life are likely to focus the patient on equally impressive antecedents: life catastrophe, an ongoing area of stress and turmoil, a serious injury, or an especially profligate form of existence are minimum events for so dire an illness outcome. More important, perhaps, than verbally directed memory recall is the direct activation of memories of past life stresses and symptom experiences by current emotional states and body sensations. Current life stresses may alter emotion and direct attention to one's body, leading to the appearance and amplification of body sensation (Scheier et al., 1979; Leventhal, 1980). Under these conditions, symptom reports could reflect past rather than current illness, a situation similar to that of phantom pain. Too little attention has been paid to the many complex ways in which situational events and emotional arousal may alter body states and create apparent correlations between past life events and current illness (see Mechanic, 1974).

Cultural concepts other than stress also play an important role in organizing illness and coping representations. Herzlich (1973) mentions beliefs such as considering the stress and filth of the city and changes due to aging as explanations for illness. These hypotheses consider contextual factors rather than focal events and are probably of special value in explaining chronic illnesses with lengthy onsets and protracted treatment. Dramatic episodes may be linked to acute conditions or seen as the precipitant of a major illness. Finally, mass media have connected dietary factors such as salt and fats to hypertension, and fats, meats, and low roughage to cancer. While these cultural norms may be based on epidemiologic evidence and have some validity, their influence on the selection of symptoms for monitoring, the antecedents to which these symptoms are attributed, and the coping responses considered appropriate goes far beyond currently verified hypotheses. An individual may attribute a high blood pressure reading to a fatty meal eaten previous to screening, or respond to a diagnosis of cancer by eating bran, taking vitamins, or becoming a strict vegetarian. There is much empirical work to be done in this area.

Cultural and social-class differences also appear in behaviors such as verbal labeling, asking questions, and seeking help. This is most dramatically illustrated in the use of mental health services. Individuals from upper socioeconomic groups whose peers accept mental health problems and services are far more likely to present emotional symptomatology, accept life situations as causes of symptoms, and utilize mental health services (Kadushin, 1968). We might argue that when a given treatment (such as consulting a psychiatrist) is part of the accepted cultural belief about illness, the act of going for treatment becomes automatic and therefore more likely to be used in situations where illness is accompanied by a high level of emotion.

Implications for Basic and Applied Epidemiology

We have pointed to a number of ways in which the manner in which people represent and cope with illness threats can influence epidemiologic data. In this section we wish to focus on a few additional issues in basic epidemiologic investigations of disease etiology and the uses of epidemiology in public policy.

Basic Research on Disease Etiology—We have identified a number of ways in which patient processing of symptom information can alter the apparent sensitivity of screening and diagnostic tests and change our estimates of disease prevalence and incidence in subgroups of populations. It is important to note that effects of this sort will differ by type of illness. Mental health epidemiology is perhaps most seriously affected by such phenomena, while data from the epidemiology of occupational disease is perhaps less so. Survey data are critical for diagnosis in mental health. Concrete image memories and their emotionally based psychophysiological reactions can generate symptom experiences that are difficult to distinguish from mental disorders produced by interactions between environmental stressors and endogenous factors. The appearance of clusters of mental-health problems within families during times of environmental stress (Kellner, 1963) may reflect an indistinguishable mixture of the problems generated by stressors or endogenous mechanisms and concrete emotional memories of distress generated by affective modeling (Schachter and Singer, 1962; Leventhal, 1979). Psychological processing of symptoms may also affect surveys used to estimate incidence and prevalence of infectious disease. The stress induced by the threat of epidemics, along with models of illness in family and friends, can stimulate emotion and concrete memory experiences of prior infectious illness. These, in turn, can generate symptom experiences that mimic those produced by actual viral transmission. Factors of this sort may account for the relatively high rate of false positives found during major flu epidemics (see Drachman et al., 1960).

There are also problems with the case control method, which matches samples of ill and well people. For example, differences between the two samples may be an effect rather than a cause of the illness (Mechanic 1974). It seems reasonable to rely on case control methods when groups differ in exposure to occupational hazards, since cancer is unlikely to lead a white collar worker to report working in an asbestos mine. Such reliance may be unwarranted, however, when it is placed on reports of concrete experiences 6 to 12 months prior to illness onset (Rahe 1972a). An illness can stimulate reports of specific prior aversive life experiences. The negative affect stimulated by an illness threat will rearouse memories linked to similar experiences of dysphoria (Janis, 1958; Leventhal, 1979, 1980). Differences of this sort may be found with increasing consistency as the control sample is more closely matched to the ill index cases on other socioeconomic, work, family, and environmental factors. With tight matching, memory differences may be the only salient, statistically detectable factors.

Another concern of basic research is depicting the natural history of illnesses, particularly for slowly developing and long-lasting chronic diseases. Explorations of this sort are heavily dependent on memory. If cultural conceptions of natural history differ for different disorders, this may greatly influence reporting. For example, mental illness appears to be attributed to characteristics of the person rather than environmental agents. As a consequence, respondents making initial visits to mental health clinics appear to reach back years in time when reporting the symptomatic onset or prior outbreak of emotionally related disturbances, while respondents making initial visits to primary care clinics for physical disorders reach back days in reporting the symptom onset.

Applications of Epidemiology to Public Policy—The problems we have just discussed translate into problems in policy formation: biases in statistics will lead to biases in the perception of problems and translate into distortions in training, facility construction, and pursuit of specific disease agents through biomedical study (for a review see Ebert, 1977; Knowles, 1977; Rogers, 1977; White, 1973).

There is, however, another and possibly more important way that psychological mechanisms alter the impact of epidemiologic findings on public policy. Epidemiologic statistics provide numerical estimates for decision making. Sound base rate data of this sort provide optimal information for policy setting. Guessing the sample mean is the best way to minimize errors when predicting individual cases! But public policy is not made in a protected arena. Statistics, the life blood of epidemiologists and planners, must compete with the opinions and judgments of elected representatives and their constituents. Unless these individuals share the epidemiologist's and planner's love of numbers, their decisions are likely to be heavily influenced by their "naive" epidemiology. The vivid images and emotions associated with a parent's, spouse's, or friend's long-term bout with a brain tumor increases the perceived importance and apparent prevalence and incidence of that illness in comparison to other human ills. Statistical data are less vivid, less meaningful, and less available to the human mind than private symptoms and observations of illness in family, friends, and well-known public figures and so less likely to win in public debate.

The findings of "commonsense epidemiology" compete, therefore, with the findings of our most reliable and valid epidemiologic studies. The more vivid and emotionally evocative the illness, the stronger the competition. This competition extends into the perception of causes and cures and the willingness to submit oneself and one's pocketbook to preventive and curative interventions. There is nothing mysterious about the rejection of water fluoridation, the ridiculing of saccharine as a cause of cancer, and the difficulty in generating wariness about risks from chemical wastes. There is nothing mysterious about the disbelief that chemical therapy can treat cancer or heart attack. In each instance, the relationship between the instigator or treatment to the disease is remote rather than immediate. Unlike an injury from a fall or surgery that removes lumps and replaces diseased arteries and kidneys, the links from cause and treatment to outcome in the prior instances are separated in time and space. The results of careful randomized trials have substantial difficulty competing against what is perceptually obvious—even when the obvious is patently false.

Fortunately, commonsense epidemiology is not entirely rigid. This is because its underlying premises are poorly developed and loosely interrelated. Well articulated systems, scientific or commonsense, show great resistance to change (Kuhn, 1970). A major challenge facing us is to characterize commonsense epidemiology more fully and discover ways of removing its biases. This can lead to improved measures of prevalence and incidence, more adequate natural histories from epidemiologic surveys, and better ways of presenting findings in the arena of public policy.

References

Antonovsky, A. (1979), *Health, Stress, and Coping*. San Francisco: Jossey-Bass.

Beecher, H.K. (1946), Pain in men wounded in battle. *Ann. Surg.*, 123:96–105.

Brown, G., Harris, T., & Peto, J. (1973), Life events and psychiatric disorders: II. Nature of causal link. *Psychol. Med.*, 3:159–176.

Carver, C.S. (1979), A cybernetic model of self-attention processes. *J. Pers. Soc. Psychol.*, 37:1251–1281.

Chapman, L. & Chapman, J. (1969), Illusory correlation as an obstacle to the use of valid psychodiagnostic signs. *J. Abnorm. Psychol.*, 74:271–280.

Chaves, J.F. & Barber, T.X. (1975), Hypnotism and surgical pain. In: *Pain:Clinical and Experimental Perspectives*, ed. M. Weisenberg. Saint Louis: Mosby, pp. 225–239.

Cleary, P. (1980), The Determinants of Psychotropic Drug Prescribing. Unpublished doctoral dissertation. University of Wisconsin, Madison, Wisconsin.

Cole, P. & Morrison, A.S. (1978), Basic issues in cancer screening. In: *Screening in Cancer*, ed. A.B. Miller. A Report of a UICC International Workshop, Toronto, Canada. Geneva, Switzerland: International Union Against Cancer.

Cupchik, G. & Leventhal, H. (1974), Consistency between expressive behavior and the evaluation of humorous stimuli: the role of sex and self-observation. *J. Pers. Soc. Psychol.*, 3:429–442.

Dewey, J. (1894), The theory of emotion: I. Emotional attitudes. *Psychol. Rev.* 1:553–569.

Dingle, J.H. (1973), The ills of man. *Sci. Amer.*, 229:77–84.

Drachman, R.H., Hochbaum, G. M., & Rosenstock, I.M. (1960), A seroepidemiologic study in two cities. In: *The Impact of Asian Influenza on Community Life*, ed. I. M. Rosenstock, G. M. Hochbaum, H. Leventhal et al. Washington, D.C.: U.S. Department of Health, Education and Welfare, Public Health Service Publication No. 766.

Ebert, R.H. (1977), Medical education in the United States. In: *Doing Better and Feeling Worse*, ed. J.H. Knowles. New York: Norton, pp. 171–184.

Engel, G. (1977), The need for a new medical model: a challenge for biomedicine. *Science*, 196:129–136.

Fabrega, H., Jr. (1973), Toward a model of illness behavior. *Med. Care*, 9:470–484.

Fabrega, H., Jr. (1975), The need for an ethno-medical science. *Science*, 189:969-975.

Fordyce, W. (1976), Behavioral concepts in chronic pain and illness. In: *The Behavioral Management of Anxiety, Depression and Pain*, ed. P.O. Davidson. New York: Brunner & Mazel, pp. 147–188.

Friedman, M., Rosenman, R.H., & Carroll, V. (1957), Changes in serum cholesterol and blood clotting time of men subject to cyclic variation of occupational stress. *Circulation*, 17:852–861.

Goldberg, I. (1974), Consideration of non-psychiatric medical settings in the delivery of mental health services. Read at the National Conference on Evaluation in Alcohol, Drug Abuse and Mental Health Programs, Washington, D.C.

Gove, W.R. & Tudor, J. (1973), Adult sex roles and mental illness. *Amer. J. Sociol.*, 78:812–835.

Gruchow, H.W. (1979), Catecholamine activity and infectious disease episodes. *J. Hum. Stress*, 5:11–17.

Gutmann, M. (1980), Personal communication, February 1.

Hackett, T.P. & Cassem, N.H. (1969), Factors contributing to delay in responding to the signs and symptoms of acute myocardial infarction. *Amer. J. Cardiol.*, 24:651–658.

Hackett, T.D. & Cassem, N.H. (1975), The psychological reactions of patients in the pre and post hospital phases of myocardial infarction. *Postgrad. Med.*, 57:43–46.

Harlow, H.F. (1959), Learning set and error factor theory. In: *Psychology: A study of a Science*, ed. S. Koch. New York: McGraw-Hill, pp. 492–537.

Herzlich, C. (1973), *Health and Illness: A Social Psychological Analysis*. New York: Academic Press.

Janis, I.L. (1958), *Psychological Stress*. New York: Wiley.

Javert, C.T. & Hardy, J.D. (1950), Measurement of pain intensity in labor and its physiologic, neurologic, and pharmacologic implications. *Amer. J. Obstet. Gynecol.*, 60:552–563.

Johnson, J.E. & Leventhal, H. (1974), Effects of accurate expectations and behavioral instructions on reactions during a noxious medical examination. *J. Pers. Soc. Psychol.*, 29:710–718.

Johnson, J.F., Leventhal, H., & Dabbs, J.M., Jr. (1971), Contributions of emotional and instrumental response processes in adaptation to surgery. *J. Pers. Soc. Psychol.*, 20:55–64.

Johnson, J. E., Rice, V.H., Fuller, S.S., & Endress, M.P. (1978), Sensory information, instruction in a coping strategy, and recovery from surgery. *Res. Nurs. Hlth*, 1:4–17.

Kadushin, C. (1968), *Why People Go to Psychiatrists*. Chicago: Aldine.

Kellner, R. (1963), *Family Ill-Health: An Investigation in General Practice*. London: Tavistock.

Kimble, G.A. & Perlmutter, L.C. (1970), The problem of volition. *Psychol. Rev.*, 77:361–383.

Knowles, J.H. (1977), *Doing Better and Feeling Worse: Health in the United States*. New York: Norton.

Kobasa, S.C. (1979), Stressful life events, personality, and health: An inquiry into hardiness. *J. Pers. Soc. Psychol.*, 37:1–11.

Kornzweig, N.D. (1967), Behavioral change as a function of fear arousal and personality. Unpublished doctoral dissertation, Yale University, New Haven, Connecticut.

Kuhn, T.S. (1970), *The Structure of Scientific Revolutions*. Chicago: University of Chicago Press.

Lazarus, R. (1966), *Psychological Stress and the Coping Process*. New York: McGraw-Hill.

Leventhal, H. (1970), Findings and theory in the study of fear communications. In: *Advances in Experimental Social Psychology*, ed. L. Berkowitz. New York: Academic Press, 5:119–186.

Leventhal, H. (1974), Emotions: a basic problem for social psychology. In: *Social Psychology: Classic and Contemporary Integrations*, ed. C. Nemeth. Chicago: Rand McNally, pp. 1–51.

Leventhal, H. (1975), The consequences of depersonalization during illness and treatment. In: *Humanizing Health Care*, ed. J. Howard & A. Strauss. New York: Wiley, pp. 119–161.

Leventhal, H. (1979), A perceptual-motor processing model of emotion. In: *Advances in the Study of Communication and Affect: Perception of Emotions in Self and Others*, ed. P. Pliner, K. Blankstein, & I.M. Spigel. New York: Plenum, 5:1–46.

Leventhal, H. (1980), Toward a comprehensive theory of emotion. In: *Advances in Social Psychology*, ed. L. Berkowitz. New York: Academic Press, pp. 139–207.

Leventhal, H., & Everhart, D. (1979), Emotion, pain and physical illness. In: *Emotions and Psychopathology*, ed. C. Izard. New York: Plenum, pp. 263–299.

Leventhal, H., Jones, S., & Trembly, G. (1966), Sex differences in attitude and behavior change under conditions of fear and specific instructions. *J. Exp. Soc. Psychol.*, 2:387–399.

Leventhal, H., Meyer, D., & Gutmann, M. (1980a), The role of theory in the study of compliance to high blood pressure regimens. In: *Working Group on Patient Compliance, Patient Compliance with Prescribed Antihypertensive Medication Regimens: A Report to the National Heart, Lung and Blood Institute*. Washington, D.C.: USDHHS, PHS, NIH, NIH Publication No. 80–2102, 1980.

Leventhal, H., Meyer, D., & Nerenz, D. (1980b), The common sense representation of illness danger. In: *Medical Psychology*, ed. S. Rachman. New York: Pergamon, 2:7–30.

Leventhal, H., & Nerenz, D. (1980), Implications of stress research for the treatment of stress disorders. In: *Stress Prevention and Management: A Cognitive Behavioral Approach*, ed. D. Meichembaum & M. Jaremko. New York: Plenum, in press.

Leventhal, H., & Niles, P. (1965), Persistance of influence for varying durations of exposure to threat stimuli. *Psychol. Rev.*, 16:223–233.

Leventhal, H., & Sharpe, E. (1965), Facial expressions as indicators of distress. In: *Affect, Cognition and Personality*, ed. S.S. Tomkins & C.E. Izard. New York: Springer, pp. 296–318.

Leventhal, H., Singer, R., & Jones, S. (1965), Effects of fear and specificity of recommendations upon attitudes and behavior. *J. Pers. Soc. Psychol.*, 2:20–29.

Leventhal, H., Watts, J.C., & Pagano, F. (1967), Effects of fear and instructions on how to cope with danger. *J. Pers. Soc. Psychol.*, 6:313–321.

Macnamara, J. (1972), Cognitive basis of language learning in infants. *Psychol. Rev.*, 79:1–13.

Mandler, G. & Watson, D.L. (1966), Anxiety and the interruption of behavior. In:

Anxiety and Behavior, ed. C.D. Spielberger. New York: Academic Press, pp. 263–288.

Marlatt, G.A. (1976), Alcohol, stress, and cognitive control. In: *Stress and Anxiety*, eds. C.D. Spielberger & I.G. Sarason. New York: Hemisphere, 3:271–296.

Mason, J.W., Buescher, E.L., Belfer, M.L., Artenstein, M.S., & Mougey, E.H. (1979), A perspective study of corticosteroid and catecholamine levels in relation to viral respiratory illness. *J. Hum. Stress*, 5:18–27.

Mechanic, D. (1963), Some implications of illness behavior for medical sampling. *New Eng. J. Med.*, 269:244–247.

Mechanic, D. (1972), Social psychologic factors affecting the presentation of bodily complaints. *New Eng. J. Med.*, 286:1132–1139.

Mechanic, D. (1974), Discussion of research programs on relations between stressful life events and episodes of physical illness. In: *Stressful Life Events: Their Nature and Effects*, ed. B.S. Dohrenwend & B.P. Dohrenwend. New York: Wiley, pp. 87–97.

Mechanic, D., & Newton, M. (1965), Some problems in the analysis of morbidity data. *J. Chron. Dis.*, 18:569–580.

Melzack, R. (1971), Phantom limb pain. *Anesthesiology*, 35:409–419.

Melzack, R. (1973), *The Puzzle of Pain*. New York: Basic Books.

Meyer, D. (1980), The effects of patients' representation of high blood pressure on behavior in treatment. Unpublished doctoral dissertation. University of Wisconsin, Madison, Wisconsin.

Meyer, D., Leventhal, H., & Gutmann, M. (1980), Symptoms in hypertension: how patients evaluate and treat them. *New Eng. J. Med.*, in press.

Miller, G.A., Galanter, E.H., & Pribram, K.H. (1960), *Plans and the Structure of Behavior*. New York: Holt.

Nathanson, C.A. (1975), Illness and the feminine role: a theoretical review. *Soc. Sci. Med.*, 9:57–62.

Nerenz, D.R. (1979), Control of emotional distress in cancer chemotherapy. Unpublished doctoral dissertation, University of Wisconsin, Madison, Wisconsin.

Pennebaker, J.W., Burnam, M.A., Schaeffer, M.A., & Harper, D.C. (1977), Lack of control as a determinant of perceived physical symptoms. *J. Pers. Soc. Psychol.*, 35:167–174.

Phillips, D.L. & Segal, B.E. (1969), Sexual status and psychiatric symptoms. *Amer. Sociol. Rev.*, 34:58–72.

Posner, M.I. (1973), *Cognition: An Introduction*. Glenview, Ill.: Scott Foresman.

Powers, W.T. (1973), Feedback: beyond behaviorism. *Science*, 179:351–356.

Rahe, R.H. (1972a), Subjects' recent life changes and their near future illness reports. *Ann. Clin. Res.*, 4:250–265.

Rahe, R.H. (1972b), Subjects' recent life changes and their near future illness susceptibility. *Adv. Psychosom. Med.*, 8:2–19.

Ringler, K. (1980), Process of Coping with Cancer Chemotherapy. Doctoral dissertation in progress. University of Wisconsin, Madison, Wisconsin.

Robinson, D. (1971), *The Process of Becoming Ill*. London: Routledge and Kegan Paul.

Rogers, D.E. (1977), The challenge of primary care. In: *Doing Better and Feeling Worse: Health in the United States*, ed. J.H. Knowles. New York: Norton, pp. 81–103.

Rogers, R.W. & Mewborn, C.R. (1976), Fear appeals and attitude change: effects of a threat's noxiousness, probability of occurrence and the efficacy of coping responses. *J. Pers. Soc. Psychol.*, 34:54–61.

Rosen, B., Locke, B., Goldberg, I., & Babigan, H. (1972), Identification of emotional disturbance in patients seen in general medical clinics. *Hosp. Commun. Psychiat.*, 23:364–370.

Ruble, D.N. (1977), Premenstrual symptoms: a reinterpretation. *Science*, 197:291–292.

Ruble, D.N. & Brooks-Gunn, J. (1979), Menstrual symptoms: a social cognition analysis. *J. Behav. Med.*, 2:171–194.

Sackett, D.L. & Haynes, R.B. (1976), *Compliance with Therapeutic Regimens*, Baltimore: Johns Hopkins University Press.

Safer, M.A., Tharpes, Q., Jackson, T., & Leventhal, H. (1979), Determinants of three stages of delay in seeking care at a medical clinic. *Med. Care*, 17:11–29.

Schachter, S. & Singer, J.E. (1962), Cognitive, social, and physiological determinants of emotional state. *Psychol. Rev.*, 69:379–399.

Scheier, M.F., Carver, C.S., & Gibbons, F.X. (1979), Self-directed attention, awareness of bodily states and suggestibility. *J. Pers. Soc. Psychol.*, 31:1576–1588.

Schwartz, G. (1979), The brain as a health care system. In: *Health Psychology*, ed. G.C. Stone, F. Cohen, & N.E. Adler. San Francisco: Jossey-Bass, pp. 549–571.

Shiffrin, R.M. & Schneider, W. (1977), Controlled and automatic human information processing: II. Perceptual learning, automatic attending, and a general theory. *Psychol. Rev.*, 84:127–190.

Shuval, J.T. (1970), *Social Functions of Medical Practice*. San Francisco: Jossey-Bass.

Simmel, M.L. (1962), The reality of phantom sensations. *Soc. Res.*, 29:337–356.

Simon, A.B., Feinleib, M., & Thompson, H.K. (1972), Components of delay in the pre-hospital phase of acute myocardial infarction. *Amer. J. Cardiol.*, 30:476–482.

Sternbach, R.A. (1974), *Pain Patients: Traits and Treatment*. New York: Academic Press.

Suchman, E.A. (1965), Stages of illness and medical care. *J. Hlth Soc. Behav.*, 6:114.

Svarstad, B. (1976), Physician-patient communication and patient conformity with medical advice. In: *The Growth of Bureaucratic Medicine*, ed. D. Mechanic. New York: Wiley, pp. 220–238.

Svebak, S. (1975), Styles in humor and social self-images. *Scand. J. Psychol.*, 16:79–84.

No Time for Depression: A Study of Help-Seeking among Mothers of Preschool Children

SUSANNAH M. GINSBERG

GEORGE W. BROWN

"Talking to other depressed women makes you even more depressed, so I expect depressed women must have that effect on doctors musn't they?"

A review of the research on sex differences in psychiatric disorder makes four points clear. First, women are *perceived* by laymen and professionals concerned with mental health to be more emotionally expressive and more likely to suffer from symptoms associated with psychiatric disorder (Broverman et al., 1970; Briscoe, 1978). Second, women are in fact more expressive than men and tend to talk more readily about themselves (Philips and Segal, 1969; Cooperstock, 1971; Horwitz, 1977, 1978). Third, women are likely to report more psychiatric symptoms and more stress in general population surveys of mental health (B.P. Dohrenwend and B.S. Dohrenwend, 1969; Mechanic and Greenley, 1976). Fourth, women are more likely to be found in psychiatric care than men, although it is unclear how far this is due to their greater overall experience of psychiatric disorder (Gove and Tudor, 1973; B.P. Dohrenwend and B.S. Dohrenwend, 1969; Greenley and Mechanic, 1976).

We will argue that the expectation and reality of women's greater emotional expressiveness documented by these studies do not serve to increase the likelihood of the recognition of depressive disorders in women by relatives, friends, and doctors. On the contrary, such beliefs exacerbate widespread tendencies to ignore depressive disorders in women. This chapter will focus on the resulting low rate of recognition of both mild and severe depressive disorders among women by relatives, friends, and doctors. The full extent of this failure to recognize depression has probably been obscured by the fact that most research has studied people already labeled by the medical profession as being psychiatrically disturbed. We will discuss our argument in relation to the literature and then with reference to our own research with 45 depressed mothers of preschool children.

Signs of depressive disorder among women (such as inexplicable crying) tend to be treated lightly by others as normal and expected components of feminine behavior. We are not concerned with disentangling the deeper psychological process of people's reaction; we will examine what motives it would be reasonable for a depressed woman to attribute to others on the basis of their reaction to her. People may realize that a woman's symptoms indicate that something is seriously amiss, but they may act as though such disturbance is normal, acceptable, and no cause for undue concern or action. This theme that depressive symptoms are seen as indicative of normal feminine behavior is one that occurs repeatedly when women are asked about the way others react to their depression. Since we will focus on women's own experience, we place particular emphasis on these beliefs. We do not argue, however, that such beliefs *in themselves* tend to lead to the lack of recognition of women's depression; rather we see these beliefs as *reinforcing* the complex and contradictory reactions that close relatives, friends, and doctors have toward depressive disorders. We believe these beliefs play a particularly important role among women with preschool children at a time in their lives when they are coping with the demands of pregnancy, small babies, and toddlers—a stage when women are often expected to experience considerable stress (Stimson, 1975).

If we are to deal with the issue of recognition of depression, it is essential to start with a clear conception of the clinical basis of this disorder. In our own research we have followed traditional and widely accepted psychiatric criteria (Finlay-Jones et al., 1980). For a woman to be diagnosed as having a *case* of depression, she must be suffering from a persistent depressed mood and at least four of the following: hopelessness, suicidal ideas or actions, weight loss, early wakening, delayed sleep, poor concentration, neglect due to brooding, loss of interest, self depreciation and lack of energy. [Information about psychiatric symptoms was obtained systematically by use of the Present State Examination (PSE). In this semistructured instrument, each symptom is defined and only symptoms reaching a certain level of severity are included (see Wing et al., 1974).] Usually more than four of these ten symptoms have been present and in every instance the person suffered from other symptoms such as worry and free-floating anxiety. Therefore in studying depression we have not been concerned with simple disorders of mood, but with a range of symptoms resulting in what can often be a severely handicapping condition.

Two features of clinical depression must be kept in mind. First, as we have just illustrated there is the ordinary nature of most of the symptoms and the fact that people may often perceive only one or two symptoms in the sufferer and not always the most severe ones. As we will see this is often abetted by the women themselves. Second, most instances of depression are brought about by major losses and disappointments (Brown and Harris, 1978). Depressed women and their relatives also often see depression in these terms. Both these components tend to distinguish depression from a condition such as schizophrenia where it is much more difficult to see the bizarre symptoms which typically occur as part of a continuum that merges with everyday emotional experience, and where precipitating events, even if they are present, will often appear trivial in the context of the severity of the illness (Brown and Birley, 1968). These two characteristics of depression obviously make it easier for symptoms to be seen as insignificant and for the possibility of psychiatric disorder to be overlooked. However, denial of disorder can also occur in response to the often more dramatic symptoms of schizophrenia. This has been convincingly documented in a study of the reaction of wives to their schizophrenic husbands (Yarrow et al., 1955). The work of Yarrow and her colleagues therefore reminds us there are likely to be powerful motives underlying the denial of an illness such as schizophrenia. It can obviously be extremely threatening to realize one's husband is "mad." The recognition that a depressed wife may be in need of psychiatric help may be equally threatening, albeit in a different way. A husband may, for example, find it more difficult to cope with the guilt he experiences over his anger toward his wife's lethargy and her general lack of interest and involvement if he defines her as psychiatrically disturbed.

There are also more situational factors that facilitate lack of recognition and the need to deny psychiatric illness where such need exists. Even with a severe psychiatric illness a person may choose to maintain a basic level of functioning in work, within the home, and outside, so that the illness does not cause a major disruption to family life (Angrist et al., 1968). A study of a group of depressed women attending a New Haven psychiatric clinic showed that even when acutely ill the women usually managed to carry on their everyday activities although at a diminished level (Weissmann et al., 1971). The impairment was not so much in actual work performance in and outside the home, but in less visible ways such as feelings of dissatisfaction and disinterest while working. The isolation of women with preschool children (the stage of life of the women in our sample) may also mean that they are less likely to have their affective disorder recognized. For example, a woman's violence toward her children, associated with her depression, may well go unnoticed if it takes place while her husband is at work and she is alone at home, as long as she does not injure the children so badly that they need medical treatment.

The way in which women themselves contribute to the process involved in the lack of recognition of their symptoms is particularly clear in their contacts with doctors in general practice. Several studies have noted how women with a large number of role obligations (such as mothers with small children) are less likely to seek help (Geertson and Gray, 1970; Brown and Harris, 1978). Complaints can be focused on others. Mechanic (1964) has indicated that mothers under stress tend to report more symptoms in their children than do those mothers not under stress, although the views of the children about their own health did not differ according to the amount of stress experienced by their mother. Other studies have shown that a mother may present a doctor with an ill child rather than with their own depression (Carne, 1966). Patients with psychiatric illness often present the general practitioner with a physical symptom, as Balint and others have shown (Balint, 1957; Goldberg and Blackwell, 1970). Women may therefore at times both attempt to conceal their depression and also seek help in an indirect fashion.

Depressed women may also have difficulty in making their needs felt by their doctor. First, since they are depressed, they may simply feel confused and unhappy and expect their problems to be recognized by the doctor. Second, many may experience difficulty in asserting themselves with male doctors, in a relationship where cultural expectations of male dominance still hold (Cooperstock and Lennard, 1979). Women suffering from clinical depression are particularly unlikely to be assertive, since the very nature of their illness will tend to increase any existing feelings of helplessness.

Several studies have suggested that doctors in general practice play a major part in this failure to detect psychiatric illness. Goldberg and Huxley (1980) have shown that, on the average, less than half of psychiatric conditions are recognized by general practitioners; but at the same time that there is a great deal of variability, with some doctors recognizing none at all and others recognizing almost every instance. Goldberg concludes, in agreement with a study by Shepherd and his colleagues (1966), that the detection of such illness depends a good deal on the orientation of the doctor—a "psychologically oriented" doctor will detect more psychiatric disturbance than one who is not. Many doctors complain that they see too much trivia (Cartwright, 1967; Mechanic, 1970).

Doctors' notions of trivia according to a study of Scottish physicians include vague emotional complaints commonly encountered in general practice (Cooperstock, 1971). Women in particular were perceived as presenting vague and trivial symptoms such as headache, fatigue, and vertigo. The assumption of course is that such trivial complaints are not of medical interest. If doctors dismiss possible signs of psychiatric disorder in this way and fail to explore them further, psychiatric disturbance of both a minor and a more serious nature may often receive little attention in general practice.

We have discussed a number of ways in which psychiatric disorder among women may remain unrecognized and untreated; although valuable, such research has so far failed to provide a convincing account of the way women experience their depression, the reaction of others to it, and the many factors of potential importance in influencing whether or not depressed women receive help and support (although work by Weissman and Paykel and Cooperstock has made an important beginning here). We hope to provide a much-needed descriptive base for research in this area, which will stimulate renewed effort to unravel factors of importance in the processes we describe.

Our research is part of a larger program concerned with affective disorders among women in Camberwell, an inner-city borough in the south of London (Brown and Harris, 1978). We have confirmed that affective disorder is common among women in urban populations when judged by responses to clinical-type interviews carried out by psychiatrists or lay persons trained in the research instrument, and that depression is ubiquitous among such disorders. One in six women in Camberwell was found to have a clear-cut affective disorder (Brown and Harris, 1978). The Camberwell research has been devoted to the development of a causal model of clinical depression and has paid relatively little attention to the response of the women themselves and their relatives and friends to the psychiatric disorder. However, the work was enough to make us aware that women often saw others, not least their husbands and general practitioners, as responding unsympathetically to their depression.

Our study of 45 depressed women (some with concomitant anxiety and phobic conditions) was based on a number of interviews with each woman in her home. The time spent with each woman was between three and seven hours. We deliberately set out to select a group of women from a larger population survey that would represent the more severely disturbed of the women defined as cases of depression in the Camberwell Survey.[1] We did this because we wanted to explore the help and support received by women whom few would question were psychiatrically ill.

Mrs. Thomas's depression is typical of the severity shown by most of the women. She had an onset of depression nine months before interview. During these nine months she lacked concentration and was unable to knit or sew, activities which she normally enjoyed. She brooded such that she sat listlessly for hours and neglected the housework sometimes for several days at a time. She lost interest in her appearance and sometimes in her children as well. Her thoughts during this period were slow and muddled. She lost fourteen pounds in the first two months due to lack of appetite and often lay awake for an hour or more before falling asleep. She reported being slowed down in her movements and taking appreciably longer to carry out every task about the house; she felt depressed, unable to smile and felt hopeless about the future.

Before we deal with the reaction of relatives, friends, and doctors to such conditions we should say a little about the women's own response to their symptoms. The women by and large suffered from severe symptoms of an emotional and somatic nature and all left us in no doubt that they found the experience extremely distressing and often scarcely tolerable—twelve, for instance, had definite

1. This was done by taking women with a child under six scoring at least 15 or over on Goldberg's 30-item General Health Questionnaire (Goldberg, 1972). Our sample was selected from women registered with a general practitioner: three different group practices were used. The total number of doctors in the three practices was twelve, but because there were a number of temporary appointments the total number of doctors seen by the women was eighteen. As part of a larger survey women were sent the questionnaire with an introductory letter from the general practitioner. When allowance is made for women *known* to have moved house the response to the questionnaire was about 75%. Only 3 of the 48 women with high GHQ scores refused to be interviewed. Women with a score of 15 or more were visited and a clinical interview was given using the shortened version of the Present State Examination (PSE) (Wing et al., 1974). The majority of women had 16 or more symptoms on the PSE while over a third had between 21 and 31 symptoms. As with the Camberwell work, careful attention was paid to the dating of the onset of symptoms. We have three scales to measure severity of depression. They are: (1) A 3-point scale based on the number of PSE symptoms: 7–15, 16–20, and 21–32. (2) A 3-point scale based on the number and type of symptoms and the extent to which a woman was incapacitated in her daily functioning by her symptoms. (3) A 3-point scale combining 1 and 2. All give much the same results in terms of factors that we will be analyzing.

suicidal ideas and seven had made a suicide attempt. In spite of the doubts that many had of benefiting from medical help (which we will describe), all but four maintained some hope of gaining support from their doctor. Whether or not the women saw themselves as suffering from a mental illness is another issue, and one which is too complex to discuss here.

Support from Family and Friends

Support was measured by the extent to which a woman said she had received sympathetic comment about her symptoms and encouragement to talk about herself. The scale covers three degrees of support: "marked," "moderate," or "little or none." Mrs. Thomas was rated as receiving "little or no support" from her husband:

I told my husband how depressed I've been feeling. He just sits in silence. If he could just talk things out and suggest something—but he doesn't.

Has he suggested you should go to the doctor?

No, he doesn't realize anything is wrong. He doesn't notice that I haven't been getting on with things!

Three quarters (27/37) of the women who were living with their husband felt that he had given "little or no support." Three quarters of the women (34/45) also felt they received little or no support from mother, other relatives such as sisters, or friends. (We always questioned about mothers and then about anybody with whom the woman said she was in regular contact.) Five reported obtaining support from both husband and someone else and in all 36% (16/45) received support from at least one person. Whether or not support was received was unrelated to the severity of the woman's depression.

It was clear from the descriptions given by the women that the behavior of others in response to their depression was often complex and contradictory. The signs and symptoms of depression are frequently ambiguous and may fluctuate a good deal. Even in a profound depression there can be periods when the sufferer appears to be well. Furthermore psychiatric disorder in a close relative or friend can arouse mixed feelings of fear, anger, and a need to deny as well as desire to help—a husband may advise his wife to go to the doctor at a point at which he feels able to give support and confront her need of help, while at other times denying there is anything wrong by explaining away her symptoms.

Given this complexity, how are we to evaluate the claim of the women that they so infrequently received support? How far is this a consequence of the fact that the very nature of their illness may have led them to misinterpret well-meant advice? Since we only spoke to the women we cannot be sure. However we did discuss in considerable detail actual incidents and it was clear that whatever the underlying motives of friends and relatives it was by and large reasonable for the woman to have construed their comments as unhelpful. The point is best conveyed by examples. Those we have selected are representative of the accounts we were given and illustrate the ways in which others tried to explain away the implications of what were often marked changes in behavior. While many of the explanations given may well have been accurate (e.g., that a woman's symptoms were due to her husband leaving her or to the birth of a child), they usually appeared to be based on the assumption that since the symptoms were an expected reaction to stress they were no cause for concern or action. This of course does not follow. A woman with clinical symptoms may still require help and support even if symptoms are a normal or expected reaction to a crisis, in much the same way as a hand that severely blisters after a burn may require medical treatment, even though such blisters are an expected normal result of the burn.

There were in fact four main ways in which symptoms such as lethargy, irritability, feelings of helplessness, loss of appetite, and fear of hitting or actually physically harming her children could be "explained away." First, they could be interpreted as a normal part of female sexuality. Depression was seen as a natural reaction to pregnancy, childbirth ("baby-blues"), the Pill, and menstruation. One woman, for example, who had recently taken an overdose was told by her mother: "It's just postnatal depression; pull yourself out of it. You can't go on feeling like that." Another, suffering from suicidal feelings and many depressive symptoms as well as severely beating her children, was told by her close friend and confidant after talking about such feelings that it was "just postnatal depression." Another with equally severe symptoms was advised by a friend that "You're bound to get this with a baby. You've got to accept it and get over it as best you can." Second, depression could be explained in terms of a minor physical complaint such as "She said she thought I was coming down with flu." One husband told his wife that she was not eating the correct food: "He thinks that I should eat more meat and drink more milk." Third, it could be explained in terms of a natural reaction to a particular stage of life or in terms of how everyone feels at times. A 28-year-old woman with a small baby who complained of lethargy, loss of interest, and violent feelings toward her child was told "You're not a young woman any more, you're married and have a child." Fourth, it could be viewed as a natural reaction to a crisis or a difficult situation. "You're bound to get depressed being in the position you're in" was a comment to a divorced woman with a 4-year-old child who had made a suicide attempt by taking an overdose of tablets. (She had vomited after the overdose and had not received medical help.) She also suffered from sleeplessness, weight loss, feelings of hopelessness, and violent feelings toward her child. Half the women reported clear and often persistent instances of such "explaining away" of symptoms illustrated by these four types of response we have described.

Women themselves at times made attempts to conceal their distress, but the majority of women who were currently living with a husband (32/37) said that they did try to talk about their depression to him. Since most were unsuccessful in gaining support, this may have contributed to a reluctance on their part to talk on later occasions about their feelings. One woman who tried to tell her husband of fears that she could seriously harm her 3-year-old child and 13-month-old baby (having already hit them so that they were clearly bruised) said that his reaction was one of incredulity:

> I tried to tell him, I felt I had to let someone know but he didn't really understand how destructive I was being to the children. I suppose he couldn't really believe I could do that (i.e., bruise the children).

Many of the women made comments along the lines: "He doesn't want to know, he doesn't want to hear" or "It goes in one ear and out the other."

The majority of husbands responded to their wives' complaints of symptoms such as suicidal ideas, feelings of helplessness, and lethargy with such comments as "You're imagining it all," "Stop being silly" or "You mustn't talk like that, there's the baby."

We have already noted the way in which relatives and friends can fail to take notice of depression if a modicum of normality is maintained in the running of the house and the care of the children. This same point was made clear by the women in our series; lapses in standards of housework (in the sense of a more untidy. grubby house, washing-up left, and so on) were felt by the women themselves to be a result of a general loss of interest, tiredness, and the like. They said, however, that their husbands on the whole did not notice as long as meals were cooked and basic housework tasks were carried out. (All but three of the women were full-time housewives.) One husband, for example, who had a basically caring warm supportive relationship with his wife attempted to reassure her when she complained of feeling depressed by saying "My dinner is always there, my washing is always done, so there can't be much wrong." We have already touched upon the question of inaccurate perception. In this kind of instance the husband's comment may well have been intended as supportive and encouraging. However, his wife experienced it as lack of understanding and a denial of her depression, as well as a denial of the feelings of dissatisfaction and frustration she felt in carrying out daily housework tasks.

While most of the women attempted to communicate their depression to their husbands, they were more likely to try to hide it from relatives and friends. Less than half the women (16/39) said they attempted to talk about their depression to their mother and this proportion was much the same even among those who saw their mother at least once a week (15/29). Shame and need to protect others, particularly mothers, were often given as reasons for this reticence. For example, one woman who felt suicidal, had lost interest in her children, was slowed down and unable to do much housework, and whose only confidant was her mother said, in explaining why she always attempted to put on a cheerful face when seeing her: "I don't want to worry her. I can talk to my Mum but I couldn't really say the things I'm saying to you. It's a bit drastic and she'd worry." Another commented: "No, I don't want to burden her: she's got enough worries."

Half the women (23/45) said they attempted to communicate their depression to their friends or a relative such as a sister. But, although they quite commonly talked to other women with small children about general feelings of distress, they rarely mentioned to anyone the depth of their depression, their fears of physically harming their children, or their feelings of hopelessness. Conversation with other mothers tended to be confined to what could comfortably be shared as familar problems. As one woman commented:

> I have talked to one friend a bit about the way I felt partly because she had done it to me. But she really had no concept of the extent of my depression or the extent of my inability to cope or my feelings of inadequacy. Perhaps this is a problem—how do you explain it to people who've never felt this way? How do you tell someone the size of the Empire State Building if they've never seen a tall building? . . . So I just said to her: 'Isn't it awful, I can't cope, and the children are horrible aren't they?' We just had a sort of discussion on that level which mothers do a lot, which doesn't actually mean 'Look I can't cope and I need help.'

Attempts made to hide symptoms of depression from close relatives and friends could clearly also mask a hope that the depression might still be shared. One woman, for example, explained how, although she tried hard to conceal her depression, she felt relieved when her friend actually noticed; but nonetheless she did not want to talk about it: "When we're taking the kids to school, she'll say 'you don't half look down Chris.' She always notices! (said with warmth). She'll say 'What's the matter?' I'll say 'nothing'."

Fear of being stigmatized was only occasionally expressed in terms such as "People look at you as if you belong in one of those mental homes if you say you're depressed." However, fears of stigmatization may have often been present as it was usually the more extreme feelings and acts of violence and aggression towards children and suicidal ideas that women tried to hide, rather than a depressed mood or feelings of lethargy which appeared often to be accepted by others as a normal state for a mother with a young child. It is worth noting that somewhat over half the women (24/45) expressed fears of seriously physically harming their children and half of these women (12/24) said that since the onset of their depression they had hit their children so hard that they had bruised them. (All said that there had been a clear change in their behaviour with onset of the condition.)

We have already commented on the complex and contradictory reactions of relatives and friends to a woman's depression. Despite the low level of overall support women received, half were nevertheless advised to seek medical advice. However, even advice to go to a doctor when given by husbands in the context of a generally unsupportive relationship could be experienced by women as a rebuff and a rejection. In all, seventeen were advised by their husbands to visit their general practitioner. As might be expected, advice seemed to be interpreted in terms of the more general framework of the relationship. Nine of the seventeen were rated as receiving a low level and eight a high level of support from their husband. Six of the nine receiving little support and none of the eight receiving a high level of support experienced the advice as rejecting. One woman with a nonsupportive relationship, who eventually went to her doctor and was referred by him to a psychiatrist, commented:

> My husband is always saying "If you've got a worry go to the doctor." He thinks (the doctor) is God actually. If we've had a row and I feel irritable, he says "Go to the doctor." That's his answer to everything.

Like what?

Well if I'm feeling a bit off colour he'll say "Go down to the doctor then." As though "Don't tell me; I can't help you." Although he could, especially last year; he could have been more understanding, more of a support. He wasn't at all.

There was, however, no association between the support a woman received for her depression from her husband or anyone else and her seeing a doctor either within the first month or first three months of onset. Because we were unable to establish the exact date at which women were told or advised to see a doctor, we have not attempted to relate advice to visiting.

This bleak account that wives gave of the support they received from relatives and friends must be seen in the context of the earlier research which suggested that risk of depression was more common in less satisfactory marriages—defined in terms of the reported ability of women to confide in their husbands (Brown and Harris, 1978). Although quite separate measures, our rating of support turned out to be almost identical with this intimacy measure. Briefly, we defined an intimate relationship with a husband as one where a woman said she talked to her husband about personal matters that were important to her. The rating was based partly on answers to direct questions in which the woman was asked to name the main person she talked to about personal things which were troubling her and partly on spontaneous comments made throughout the interview (see Brown and Harris, 1978, pp. 175–179).

Ten of the twelve women reporting a currently intimate tie with their husband also reported receiving a high level of support from him compared to only one of the 25 without such an intimate tie. This suggests that given a satisfactory long-term relationship, a husband is much more likely to react supportively to his wife's depression. It is also possible that women developing depression have in general less satisfactory social contacts with relatives and friends than women in general (see Miller and Ingham, 1976; Henderson et al., 1978; Brown and Harris, 1978). In other words the support received from husbands, relatives, and friends by women in our series would not necessarily be found to be the same if risk of depression were randomly distributed in the population. Relatively poor supportive ties of all kinds almost certainly increase risk of depression in the first place.

Support from the General Practitioner

It is essential to recognize that seeing a doctor is in no way synonymous with the depression being treated. In fact, although all but three of the 45 women visited their general practitioner during an episode of depression, only just over half (23/42) had their depression acknowledged by him at some point. We included as *acknowledgment* any recognition, however minimal, that a woman might be suffering from psychiatric disorder. For example, a doctor who said a woman's rash was due to "nerves" and the consultation ended there with no further questions on his part or comment by the woman, was considered to have acknowledged her depression. Similarly a woman would be considered to have had her depression acknowledged if her doctor prescribed psychotropic drugs after she had said she felt tense, but did not talk to her about other symptoms or any problems she might have. [It is interesting to note Raynes's (1979) finding that the decision to prescribe psychotropic drugs in general practice tends to be made in the context of recognizing psychological and social problems rather than making a psychiatric diagnosis. Our definition for acknowledgment of psychiatric disorder is consistent with this.] Our rating of the severity of depression did not relate to whether or not the depression was acknowledged, nor did support received from husband or others relate to the condition being acknowledged.

The length of depression at the time of interview ranged from two months to two and a half years with a median length of four months. During the length of their depression all but three of the 45 women had consulted for themselves or their children and all but two of these consulted at some point for themselves alone. The number of visits ranged from 1 to 18 with a median of 3 and not surprisingly were quite highly correlated with lengths of episode ($r = 0.59$). The proportion having their depression acknowledged, in the sense we have defined it, increased from just under a quarter (6/28) among those attending in the first month to about a half among those who attended at any point before our interview (23/42). The chances of a woman's depression being acknowledged remained constant at 1 in 4 until she had either made 4 visits or the episode had lasted over 12 months: 81% (17/21) of women with 4 or more visits or an episode of over 12 months had had their depression acknowledged compared with a quarter (6/24) of the remainder ($p < 0.02$). The number acknowledged in terms of frequency of visits and lengths of episode is shown in table 1.

So far our findings are consistent with the conclusions of Goldberg and Blackwell (1970) and Shepherd and his colleagues (1966) discussed earlier, that recognition of psychiatric illness in general practice depends on the doctor's orientation—the more psychiatri-

TABLE 1

Number of Women Whose Depression Was Acknowledged by a General Practitioner (Measured by Length of Episode and Number of Visits to See a Doctor during the Episode)

Number of Visits	1–3	Length of Episode (Months) 4–6	7–9	10–12	13+	Total
0	0/3					0/ 3
1		2/ 6[a]	0/1	0/1		2/ 8
2	1/2	1/ 4			1/ 1	3/ 7
3		2/ 3	0/4		1/ 2	3/ 9
4		2/ 2	2/2	0/1	1/ 1	5/ 6
5+		1/ 1	0/1	2/2	7/ 8	10/12
Total	1/5	8/16	2/8	2/4	10/12	23/45

[a] Number of women whose depression was acknowledged by a general practitioner (number to left of slash) out of a total number of women in the particular sample (number to right of slash). In this case, only 2 (out of a total of 6) women who had made 1 visit to see a doctor and whose depression had lasted 4–6 months had their depression acknowledged.

cally orientated perceiving more disturbance. However, as we have noted, women themselves also play a part in concealing their depression. We have already described some of the ways women attempt to hide their depression from family and friends, and this kind of ambivalence can also be seen in the way they behave with their doctor. According to their accounts only a quarter (10/42) presented the doctor with their depression in a direct way on their first contact after onset. (Our definition of direct presentation of depression included such symptoms as "bad nerves" or violence toward children based on the argument that these type of "symptoms" clearly indicate the possibility of psychiatric disorder.) Women were just as likely to present the doctor with a sick child or a physical symptom. It is clear that those who did not present the doctor directly with their depression were unlikely to get help. Only four of the 32 who did not present directly on their first visit after onset had their depression acknowledged during this visit compared with nine of the ten women who did. The proportions remain of much the same order when the whole period is taken into account (i.e., from onset to time of interview).[2]

2. Women were asked what the first thing was that they presented to the doctor after they had entered the consulting room. A symptom mentioned later in the consultation was not included as a presenting symptom because of the possibility of it

A major reason why so many women did not present the doctor directly with their depression appears to be that depression was seen as an inappropriate complaint to bring to a general practitioner. Just over half (24/45) the women said they felt that doctors are there to deal with physical symptoms; two-thirds (31/45) that doctors do not have time to talk, and a similar proportion (30/45) that they only treat depression with drugs.[3]

Attitudes at times appeared to have been influenced by previous experiences of consulting doctors. Several women referred to visits they had made, sometimes years before, where they had felt the doctor had been unresponsive about a previous episode of depression. Television and women's magazines were also referred to by women as influencing their ideas about the doctor's role. For example, women referred to television programs they had seen in which doctors talked of patients who wasted their time complaining of nerves and trivial symptoms and who expected them to wave a magic wand. Such women felt discouraged from visiting their doctor to discuss their depression.

All but three of the women attributed their depression to social and psychological difficulties (bad housing, unhappy marriage, and the like) and believed that drugs alone would not help. In fact just over half (22/42) of the women who visited their doctor were at some point prescribed a psychotropic drug and it was rare for any other form of help to be offered. Although prescribing a psychotropic drug was one criterion of a doctor's acknowledgment, it is worth pointing out that all but one of those whose depression was acknowledged in our terms (22/23) received a prescription for such a drug. This should be contrasted to the belief expressed by three-quarters of the women (33/45) that talking about their depression

---

having been mentioned in response to the doctor's questioning. However, even if *anything* said at the interview is taken into account our results change very little.

The proportion of women whose depression was acknowledged among those not presenting their depression directly rose from 13% (4/32) at the first visit to 24% (6/25) when the whole period was taken into account; the proportion acknowledged among those presenting directly remained the same—90% (9/10) and 94% (16/17) respectively.

3. It is interesting to note that neither the large-scale study in Camberwell (Brown and Harris, 1978) nor our present work shows any clear social-class differences in treatment seeking. Another recent study on patients with migrane has also found no class differences in contacting the doctor (Fitzpatrick, 1980). However, it is important to point out that the Camberwell study showed a very large relation between social class and those treated by psychiatrists (Brown and Harris, 1978; Hurry and Brown, 1980).

and their problems would be the best way they could be helped. A prescription for psychotropic drugs tended to be seen as a rejection if it was not given in the context of what was perceived by the women as a supportive attitude, where the doctor gave time and listened sympathetically.Three-quarters (17/22) of those women prescribed such drugs saw it as a rejection. The actual experience of the women who presented their doctor directly with their depression is consistent with the expectations of those who felt it was pointless to do so (and did not) because they would receive what they felt to be inappropriate help—the following are typical comments:

If I went to the doctor he would just write a prescription. When I feel depressed pills aren't going to stop what's making me depressed. When you talk about it, there's a way out. It don't seem so bad.

If I told the doctor I was depressed he would give me a tonic or some pills.

How would you have felt about that?

I would think that's not why I'd gone.

What would you want?

Just talking to really.

Such misgivings on the part of many of the women often went with hope that the doctor would give them time and listen to them. Despite low expectations most went to see their doctor making several visits during their depression. In other words, women tested their doctor's reaction. This was done by presenting him with what they felt to be an acceptable symptom, but with hope that the doctor himself would probe further and discover the "real" problem. Alternatively women hoped for some unspoken sign, a friendly look, an unhurried manner, which would encourage them to mention their depression. It was difficult to establish the reason for each and every visit, particularly as the women themselves so often held conflicting feelings about whether or not to mention their depression. It was clear, however, that at some point almost all had wanted to discuss their depression. (All but four were quite explicit about this and our general feeling is that they held some hope of discussing their depression on most of the visits they made.)

As we have said, our definition of a doctor's acknowledgment of depression refers to a minimum recognition on his part that a woman may be suffering from psychiatric disorder. We have said enough to convey that such acknowledgment was not the same as satisfactory treatment in the woman's eyes. There are a number of possible ways of measuring satisfaction with treatment. A woman's answer to a question about satisfaction can be taken, spontaneous expressions of satisfaction and dissatisfaction can be taken, or the investigator can impose his own standards according to what the woman had said occurred with the doctor. We have relied mainly on a fourth approach, based on criteria that the women as a whole most frequently mentioned when discussing satisfactory contact. The criteria we took were whether the doctor had asked about symptoms other than the presenting symptom, whether he asked if a woman had any problems, and whether he had suggested that she return to see him, either by making a definite appointment, or by indicating that she would be welcome to return if she wanted to. Taking women who reported at least two of these three criteria, only nine received at any point satisfactory treatment. However, even when we ignore what occurred between the woman and the doctor and rely on what the woman said and on spontaneous comments she made throughout the interview when talking about treatment, much the same result is obtained.

Since our study indicates less satisfaction on the part of patients in general practice than do other published reports (see Locker and Dunt, 1978) further comment about our measure of reported satisfaction may be useful. As already noted, we did not rely on answers to standard questions about satisfaction and dissatisfaction but rather on any relevant comment made throughout a lengthy interview. We took into account not only what was said, but how it was said, paying particular attention to tone of voice. This approach to the measurement of feeling expressed in an interview has been shown to be highly reliable (Brown and Rutter, 1966; Rutter and Brown, 1966) and a convincing case can be made for its construct validity (e.g. Brown et al., 1972; Vaughn and Leff, 1976). It is known that such measures can differ markedly from those obtained by asking direct questions. For example, Oakley (1974) has shown that there is a large association between social class and a woman's expressed satisfaction in answer to a direct question about whether or not she enjoys housework. However she went on to show that this association entirely disappeared when satisfaction was rated in terms of the womens' spontaneous comments about housework throughout a lengthy interview. It appears in this instance at least that it is what women feel they *ought* to like that is picked up by standard questions about satisfaction and dissatisfaction, working-class women being more likely to identify with housework. In a similar way it is possible that most women feel they *ought* to feel satisfied with their doctor.

Of course, both positive and negative feeling can be expressed and our ratings therefore referred to the *predominant* feeling throughout the interview. We also took into account comments made about *any* visit made during the course of the depression. Using this approach thirteen of the 42 women (31%) were rated as "satisfied" if we include four who said they felt satisfied although none of our three criteria of an effective consultation had been met. These four women all expressed low expectations of help the doctor could give; all presented with physical symptoms and said that they felt reasonably satisfied with the doctor's response to the symptoms they presented. Their satisfaction therefore appeared to reflect low expectations about the help that could be gained from seeing a doctor about their depression.

Of the remaining 29 women rated dissatisfied, eight reported one positive experience with the doctor amid, or at the end, of a series of negative experiences. Overall these women clearly felt their visits to the doctor had been unsatisfactory. Two of the eight had a satisfactory visit after having changed their general practitioner after they had moved house; another three had a positive experience in the middle of a series of visits, but saw different doctors after this. The remaining three of the eight had a satisfactory encounter on the last visit they made, one being after thirteen visits. [The inclusion of these eight women would bring the total of satisfied women at the most conservative estimate to exactly half of those attending their general practitioner (21/42). However, since our rating of satisfaction is based on the *predominant* feelings that women had about their interaction with the doctor during their depression we excluded these eight women from the total number rated as satisfied.

One common complaint has not so far been mentioned. All the women belonged to a group practice and told us that they were usually unable to see the doctor of their choice if they wanted a consultation within a day or two. They often complained of this and of the fact that if they visited on more than one occasion for their depression they usually saw a different doctor. (Thirty-four of the 42 women visiting their doctor during the course of their depression made more than one visit. Twenty-one of these saw more than one doctor and twelve saw three or more doctors.) The underlying reasons for this situation are undoubtedly complex but it seems sufficient in this chapter to make the point that well over half the women spontaneously mentioned this as a problem.[4]

4. Seven of the 45 women had seen a social worker during their illness. Four of the seven had been referred to psychiatric outpatients and then referred to a social worker by a psychiatrist. Six women in all received treatment from a psychiatrist.

During the remainder of this chapter we will describe in more detail a few typical examples of the way the women experienced their contacts with the doctor. First, we will illustrate instances of a doctor's acknowledgment in the minimal sense in which we have defined it. Second, instances where depression was not acknowledged, and third, instances of "satisfactory" contacts.

Mrs. Smith's experience is typical of the kind of contact many of the women had with their doctor. She suffered from tiredness, tension, and restlessness, and had difficulty in concentrating. She brooded such that she neglected the house and her child. She lost interest in reading or watching television, activities which used to interest her. She had difficulty in getting off to sleep at night, often lying awake for an hour or more. She felt very depressed most of the time and was also suicidal. Her thoughts were muddled and slow and her movements were retarded. During the eighteen months of her depression she made three visits to her doctor but on no occasion did she mention her depression as a reason for her visiting, illustrating the way women can test the doctor's reaction. On the first visit she presented her doctor with her baby's hernia, on the second with her baby's rash, and on the third she asked about contraception. Mrs. Smith's experience also illustrates an instance of a contact with the doctor where depression was acknowledged. At interview she was still markedly depressed. She said she had wanted to talk to her doctor about her depression ever since it began eighteen months before the interview, but she doubted he could do anything for her, and she questioned whether it was appropriate for her to mention her depression in the first place. (Her husband had kept telling her to go.) Eventually some two months after onset she made an appointment for her baby and decided she would mention her own depression.

I just went to the doctor for the baby and my husband kept saying "tell the doctor about your depression; why don't you see a doctor?" I said "Well I'll mention it while I'm there and see what he says (about me)."

I said "I don't see what the doctor can do." My husband wanted me to go so I said "O.k. I'll do it." But the doctor just didn't want to know. I said to

---

Three as inpatients and three as outpatients. Five had been referred by their general practitioner and one was seen after she had been admitted to hospital as an emergency after an overdose. One woman contacted a private psychotherapist, independently of her general practitioner. All the women who received treatment from a psychiatrist or social worker also had their depression acknowledged by their doctor. Such help therefore supplemented rather than substituted support and recognition from the general practitioner.

the doctor I was feeling very depressed and very tired and life was hard to cope with and my husband wanted me to discuss it with you while I was over here to see what you would say to it. I just told him I thought "the rest is up to you." I mean it's a bit hard to go over there and say you're depressed. I feel far happier saying I've got a pain in my arm.

Although Mrs. Smith, unlike many other women, did actually take the step of mentioning her depression, she waited for the doctor to show an interest and explore her problems. However, he did not do so and the matter went no further. She "tested" the doctor before exposing the full extent for her symptoms. She complained that:

The doctor said "It'll pass; you'll get over it!" He was completely disinterested. He just wanted to write me out a prescription.

Eleven months after this visit, still in much the same state, Mrs. Smith returned and saw a different doctor. She presented him with her baby's rash and a month later she visited again, seeing another doctor for contraceptive advice. On neither of these occasions did she mention her depression nor was it picked up by the doctors. When we interviewed her eighteen months after onset she said that she would like help but was convinced that doctors were not interested in "mental illness":

The doctors over there aren't interested if you're mentally ill and you've got stresses and strains. They're only interested if you've got something physically wrong with you. This is the impression they give. You don't really like to keep bothering them when you're not physically ill.

Others were even more explicit than Mrs. Smith about the way in which they sought an "excuse" to visit the doctor. A third of the women (15/45) actually said they waited until their child became ill before going. One woman whose depression was not acknowledged by the doctor described fears of wasting his time and her belief that the doctor would only provide Valium which she did not want to take. She admitted, however, that she often wished that her 3-year-old child would become ill so she could go along to the surgery: "Sometimes I find myself thinking I wish she wasn't well; then I could go to the doctor, then I could take her and ask him about myself." This woman had been depressed for seven months and had visited her doctor three times—once presenting with a pain in her breast (for which the doctor could find no cause) and once complaining that she felt tense before her periods. The week before interview she had taken her child to the doctor with a mild earache.

On no occasion did she mention she was depressed, nor did the doctor on the first two visits she made ask her if she had any problems or was suffering from further symptoms such as loss of sleep or appetite. (She had lost a good deal of weight and had difficulty in sleeping.)

It is not only what doctors say that influence women: nonverbal signs were also readily interpreted either as a license to talk or as a clear signal that the doctor was not interested. Fiddling with a prescription pad, no looking at his patient, not sitting back in his chair, were all interpreted as signs of a doctor's unwillingness to listen attentively.

They seem to carry on doing something while you're talking.

Like what?

Like fiddling about with papers or opening the door while you're talking. I've had that happen to me.

What did that make you feel?

Right annoyed!

Another woman explained why she had not mentioned her depression while consulting for a swelling stomach: "He didn't seem to be interested. He didn't look friendly. He didn't make me feel as if he was friendly enough to sit and listen."

She did, however, discuss her depression the following week when returning with a cough. On this occasion she saw another doctor who appeared friendly and unhurried: She said "He seemed more relaxed. He looked at you when he talked as if he had more time."

On this occasion she felt able to talk about her marital problems and received advice to consult a marriage guidance counsellor. The doctor did not ask her directly whether she had any problems, but she felt he indicated concern by his manner and willingness to listen. This encounter was rated as "satisfactory" in terms of our three criteria.

Mrs. Xavier is another example of a woman who had a "satisfactory" encounter with her doctor. Five of the nine women experiencing such an encounter felt that it was not so much the doctor's giving concrete advice (such as to go to a marriage guidance counsellor) but the fact of his giving time, listening, and indicating concern that had been helpful. Mrs. Xavier went to her doctor having felt severely depressed and suicidal since her husband had left her. She said: "You can talk to him about anything. That's what helps. You feel when you talk to him he's taking it in. He's such an understanding doctor. He's a good doctor."

The doctor prescribed drugs. He also spent half an hour with her and discussed problems she had with her husband. He told her to return when she felt she wanted to see him again. When interviewed six weeks after this encounter Mrs. Xavier was still depressed though she no longer felt suicidal. She said she had not felt the need to return to her doctor because "I think of what he said and it is pulling me through. I know I can go and see him whenever I want and he will always listen so I don't feel the need to go back at the moment."

It is beyond the scope of this study to look at how the doctors themselves varied in their reactions to women. In reviewing the literature and discussing the reaction of family and friends we referred to the expectations held in our society that women, and particularly mothers of small babies and children, are prone to suffer from depressive symptoms such as crying, tension, and the like. It may well be that the less psychiatrically oriented doctors who, as Goldberg and others have indicated, perceive less psychiatric illness, may be the ones who are inclined to perceive women's depression (in so far as they perceive it at all) as natural and normal. Certainly many of the women felt that the doctor had explained away their depression or their symptoms by stating that it was normal for a woman in a particular situation. One woman, for example, suffering from sleeplessness, suicidal thoughts, and fears of physically harming her child, told her doctor she felt agitated, could not relax, and was afraid she would hurt her children. She also told him that she was constantly in tears. His response was "How can you expect to be calm, you've got four children." Another was given a prescription for Valium before she felt she had explained her symptoms clearly: "I said what's that for?" He said "Take these—all you divorced women up there (a tower block) take these."

As we have stated, the assumption underlying the attitude that women's depression is "normal" in certain situations is that the depression itself does not merit much attention. The prescribing of psychotropic drugs is a common response on the part of general practitioners to women's emotional complaints and this becomes a "normal" solution for a "normal" problem.

Our study clearly shows that despite a few exceptions women's clinical depression in the community remains largely untreated and unacknowledged. Figure 1 summarizes the main quantitative findings:

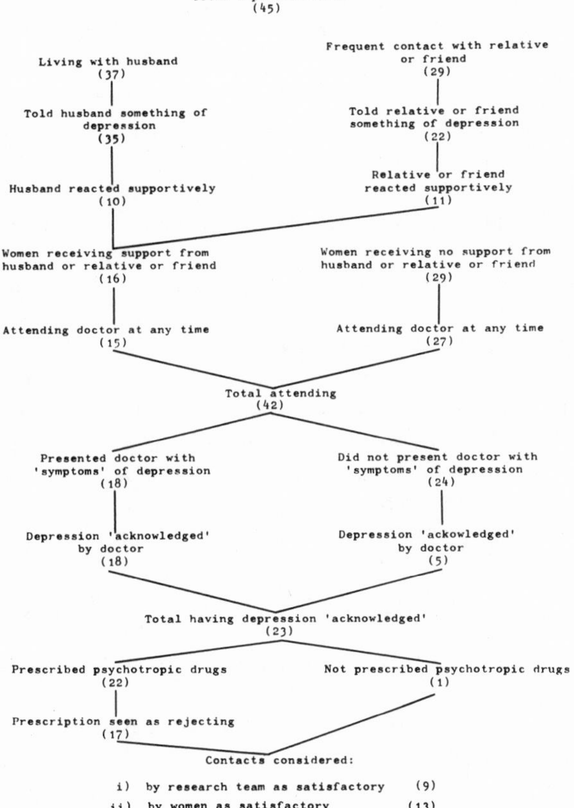

Conclusions

We are aware that by talking only to depressed women we risk appearing to present the issues in Manichaean terms and that any biases that occur in their accounts will tend to support their point of view. Psychiatric disorder can be extraordinarily difficult to live with, and the problems experienced by husbands and others in coping with a depressed woman should not be minimized. What then can be said in favor of our approach? It is useful to keep several considerations in mind in evaluating the reports the women gave us. First what *actually occurred* when, for example, a wife reports that her husband irritably told her to stop making such a fuss and to pull herself together. Second, the *wider context* of the incident—namely that her husband reacted so irritably only after his wife had constantly phoned him at work and had become increasingly dependent and demanding. Third, the woman's *feelings* about what had occurred—her distress when her husband treated her fears of harming her child with incredulity.

We suspect that the accounts we have collected are reasonably accurate in terms of our first and third points—that is, in terms of what actually occurred and the woman's feelings about this. However, the women's accounts often fall short in their description of our second point concerning the broader context of the incidents. But detailed interviewing of other participants would not necessarily deal with this. What a person chooses to see as relevant is bound to be highly selective and it is hopeless to expect as a matter of course that such accounts will average out into one that is correct. Other perspectives would, however, probably increase our sympathy for everyone involved. Knowledge of what a husband has experienced and his anger at his wife's increasing dependence would give a broader context in which to view what happened and would perhaps be sufficient to remind us that we ourselves might not behave very differently in the same situation.

General practitioners must equally find it difficult to cope with the psychiatric disorder of their patients: their training has usually ill-equipped them for the task of tackling problems which fall outside traditional areas of medicine.

Turning to the results of our study, three striking points emerge. First, although almost all the women saw their doctor during depression, only about half had their depression acknowledged. Furthermore this acknowledgment usually consisted of no more than a minimal recognition that a woman might be suffering from a psychiatric disorder with no exploration on the part of the doctor of the full range of symptoms or difficulties that might have led to them. It should also be noted that in almost every instance where the doctor acknowledged the depression, a prescription for psychotropic drugs was given. Our second main point is the low level of satisfaction reported by the women compared with other studies on doctor-patient relationships and our third main point, the extent to which family and friends do not recognize that a woman may be in need of help.

These findings must be seen in the context of widely held beliefs that it is normal and expected for women, particularly mothers of young children, to suffer from symptoms associated with depressive disorders such as constant crying. As we have said, the assumption underlying such expectations is that because symptoms associated with depressive disorder are considered normal in women they are not considered to be cause for undue concern or to require help. Thus in spite of these widely held beliefs it is difficult for women to have their depression unequivocally acknowledged. A recurrent theme of the interviews was the way in which family and friends and even the general practitioner explained away and normalized the woman's condition. We have made clear that the beliefs surrounding the assumption that women are naturally more emotionally expressive serve to facilitate the role of more complex and fundamental motives that exist for disregarding and denying the depressive disorder of a close relative, friend, or patient. Although we place particular importance on such cultural beliefs, we believe it would be simplistic to see them as acting along to produce the picture of lack of support we have documented—we see such beliefs as reinforcing widespread tendencies to deny psychiatric disorder.

If, as we have argued, our description of such neglect is reasonably accurate how representative are our findings? The fact that women who become depressed are likely to have poorer marital relationships in the first place (and perhaps social support in general) must also be borne in mind when interpreting the accounts we have presented. It may be of some consolation to the reader that if risk of depression were random, matters would probably not appear to be as bleak.

The doctors in our sample are probably reasonably representative. Three group practices in outer London were asked to collaborate in our work and all were generous enough to allow us to use their records to select a random list of names. We therefore did not cover single and joint partnerships, but doctors in group practices already form almost two-thirds of doctors in outer London. The movement toward such group practices is steadily increasing and the experience of the women in our sample, particularly in terms of the difficulties they had in seeing the doctor of their choice at short notice, may well become increasingly typical.

Our final point must concern the practical issue of treatment. It is clear that the difficulty in coping with a depressed person, and the anxiety and anger it must arouse, does not rest with family and friends alone. The traditional training of medical students and the inadequate facilities with which many doctors work in general practice can clearly hinder the general practitioner in treating the psychiatrically disturbed patient. If social and psychological problems were seen as a legitimate and central part of medicine and empathetic listening an important beginning in the hard task of tackling such problems, doctors might well feel more reward from dealing with their depressed patients. As long as listening and encouraging a patient to talk about his or her problems is seen as a peripheral aspect of medicine, then most doctors can only feel that time spent in this way is time wasted on trivia, to the detriment of real medical practice. The attachment of counselors or social workers to general practice on a much wider scale than at present might alleviate some of the doctor's load, while providing the kind of support and help which depressed women themselves feel they most need. The exact form provision should take, the effect it would have, and the kind of patient who could benefit from it are as yet unclear (Cooper et al., 1975; Shepherd et al., 1979). What is clear, however, is the presence of a widespread problem in dealing with psychiatric disorder in general practice, and this in itself justifies serious attempts to evaluate the efficacy of different modes of intervention.

Acknowledgments

The research was supported by a grant from the Medical Research Council.

We are extremely grateful to the general practitioners who collaborated with us. We are also grateful to our colleagues for helpful criticism of earlier drafts of this paper. We would particularly like to mention Claire Baron, Ruth Cooperstock, Ray Fitzpatrick, Jim Greenley, Tirril Harris, and Arlene McLaren. Finally and most importantly we owe our thanks to the women who generously gave their time to talk to us.

References

Angrist, S., Lefton, M., Dinitz, S., & Pasamanick, B. (1968), *Women after Treatment: A Study of Former Mental Patients and their Normal Neighbors.* New York: Appleton-Century-Crofts.

Balint, M. (1957), *The Doctor, His Patient and the Illness.* London: Tavistock.

Briscoe, M.E. (1978), Sex Differences in perception of illness and expressed life satisfaction. *Psychol. Med.*, 8:339–345.

Brown, G.W. & Birley, J.L.T. (1969), Crises and life changes and the onset of schizophrenia. *J. Hlth Soc. Behav.*, 9:203–214.

Brown, G.W., Birley, J.L.T. & Wing, J.K. (1972), Influence of family life on the course of schizophrenic disorders: a replication. *Brit. J. Psychiat.*, 130:1–18.

Brown, G.W. & Harris, T.O. (1978), *Social Origins of Depression: A study of Psychiatric Disorder in Women.* London: Tavistock.

Brown, G.W. & Rutter, M. (1966), The measurement of family activities and relationships: a methodological study. *Hum. Relat.*, 19:241–263.

Broverman, I.K., Broverman, D.M., Clarkson, F.E., Rosenkratz, P.S., & Vogel, S.R. (1970), Sex role stereotypes and clinical judgements of mental health. *J. Consult. Clin. Psychol.*, 34:1–7.

Carne, S. (1966), The influence of the mother's health on her child. *Proc. Royal Soc. Med.*, 59:1013–1014.

Cartwright, A. (1967), *Patients and Their Doctors.* London: Routledge and Keegan Paul.

Cooper, B., Harwin, B.G., Depla, C., & Shepherd, M. (1975), Mental health care in the community: an evaluative study. *Psychol. Med.*, 5:372–380.

Cooperstock, R. (1971), Sex differences in the use of mood modifying drugs: an explanatory model. *J. Hlth Soc. Behav.*, 12:238–244.

Cooperstock, R. (1974), *Social Aspects of the Medical Use of Psychotropic Drugs.* Ontario: Addiction Research Foundation.

Cooperstock, R. & Lennard, H.L. (1979), Social meanings of tranquilizer use. *Sociol. Hlth Ill.*, 3:331–347.

Dohrenwend, B.P. & Dohrenwend, B.S. (1969), *Social Status and Psychological Disorder.* New York: Wiley.

Finlay-Jones, R., Brown, G.W., Duncan-Jones, P., Harris, T.O., Murphy, E., & Prudo, R. (1980), Depression and anxiety in the community: replicating the diagnosis of a case. *Psychol. Med.*, 10:455–464.

Fitzpatrick, R. (1980), *Personal communication.*

Geertson, H.R. & Gray, R.M. (1970), Familistic orientation and inclination toward adopting the sick role. *J. Marr. Fam.*, 32:638–646.

Goldberg, D.P. (1972), *The Detection of Psychiatric Illness by Questionnaire.* London: Oxford University Press.

Goldberg, D.P. & Blackwell, B. (1970), Psychiatric illness in general practice: a detailed study using a new method of case identification. *Brit. Med. J. ii*: 439–443.

Goldberg, D.P. & Huxley, P. (1980), *Mental Illness in the Community: The Pathway to Psychiatric Care.* London: Tavistock.

Gove, W.R. & Tudor, J. (1973), Adult sex roles and mental illness. *Amer. J. Sociol.*, 78:812–835.

Greenley, J.R. & Mechanic, D. (1976), Social selection for seeking help for psychological problems. *J. Hlth Soc. Behav.*, 17:249–262.

Henderson, S., Byrne, D.G., Duncan-Jones, P., Adcock, S., Scott, R., & Steele, G.P. (1978), Social bonds in the epidemiology of neurosis: a preliminary communication. *Brit. J. Psychiat.*, 132:463–466.

Horwitz, A. (1977), The pathways into psychiatric treatment: some differences between men and women. *J. Hlth Soc. Behav.*, 18:169–178.

Horwitz, A. (1978), Family, kin and friends networks in psychiatric help seeking. *Soc. Sci. Med.*, 12:297–304.

Hurry, L.J. & Brown, G.W. (1980), Contacting a psychiatrist. Unpublished manuscript.

Locker, D. & Dunt, T. (1978), Theoretical and methodological issues in sociological studies of comsumer satisfaction with medical care. *Soc. Sci. Med.*, 12:253–292.

Mechanic, D. (1964), The influence of mothers on their children's health and behavior. *Pediatrics.*, 33:444–453.

Mechanic, D. (1970), Frustration among British practitioners. *J. Hlth Soc. Behav.*, 11:87–104.

Mechanic, D. & Greenley, J.R. (1976), The prevalence of psychological distress and helpseeking in a college student population. *Soc. Psychiat.*, 11:1–14.

Miller, P.M. & Ingham, J.G. (1976), Friends, confidants and symptoms. *Soc. Psychiat.*, 11:51–58.

Oakley, A. (1974), *The Sociology of Housework.* London: Martin Robertson.

Phillips, D.L. & Segal, B.E. (1969), Sexual Status and psychiatric symptoms. *Amer. Sociol. Rev.*, 34:58–72.

Raynes, N.V. (1979), Factors affecting the prescribing of psychotropic drugs in general practice consultations. *Psychol Med.*, 9:671–679.

Rutter, M., & Brown, G.W. (1966), The reliability of family life and relationships in families containing a psychiatric patient *Soc. Psychiat.* *1*:38–53.

Shephard, M., Cooper, B., Brown, A.C., & Kalton, G. (1966), *Psychiatric Illness in General Practice.* London: Oxford University Press.

Shepherd, M. & Harwin, B.G., Delpa, C., & Cairns, V., (1979), Social work and the primary care of mental disorder. *Psychol. Med.* 9:661–679.

Stimson, G. (1975), Women in a doctored world. *New Society*, 32:267–269.

Vaughn, C.E. & Leff, J.P. (1976), The influence of family and social factors on the course of psychiatric illness: a comparison of schizophrenic and depressed neurotic patients. *Brit. J. Psychiat.*, 129:125–139.

Weissman, M.M. & Paykel, E.S. (1974), *The Depressed Woman: A Study of Social Relationships.* Chicago: University of Chicago Press.

Weissman, M.M. Siegel, R., & Klerman, G.L. (1971), The social role performance of depressed women: comparisons with a normal group *Amer. J. Orthopsychiat.*, 41:390–404.

Wing, J.K., Cooper, J.E., & Sartorious, N. (1974), *The Measurement and Classification of Psychiatric Symptoms: An Instruction Manual for the Present State Examination and Catego Programme.* London: Cambridge University Press.

Yarrow, M., Schwartz, C., Murphy, H., & Deasy, L. (1955), The psychological meaning of mental illness in the family. *J. Soc. Iss.*, 11:12–24.

Psychosocial Disorder in Primary Medical Care

PAUL WILLIAMS

MICHAEL SHEPHERD

Medical care in Great Britain is organized on a two-echelon system (Querido, 1962), with primary health care being provided by National Health Service general practitioners. Ninety-eight percent of the population is registered with a general practitioner, 60–70% consult him at least once in any given year, and the proportion of the population who have not consulted for two years or longer is only about 10%. Thus, such a general practitioner, by virtue of his position as the purveyor of primary medical care to a population, is well-placed to monitor psychosocial disorder in the general population, and to identify those patients whose symptoms are serious enough to warrant treatment. Also, to the extent that he can be regarded as a personal physician, he enjoys the major asset of direct access to the medical history and social background of his patients. Often, his assessment of any one patient is based not only on observations made at a single consultation, but also on professional contact with the patient and his family which extends back over many years. Moreover, his special relationship with his patients confers on him the unique advantage of gaining their cooperation and in eliciting personal information that may be essential for a realistic appraisal of their complaints.

In 1971, there were just over 20,000 general practitioners in England and Wales, each looking after an average of 2,400 patients (Hicks, 1976). Of these doctors, 20% were in practice on their own ("single-handed practitioners"), while the remainder worked in partnership with one or more other doctors ("a practice"). A relatively recent trend in British general practice has been the development of the Health Centre, in which a number of general practitioners work as members of a "primary health-care team" with other professionals (e.g., nurses, health visitors, social workers), in purpose-built premises fully equipped with supporting services and ancillary personnel. It is thus similar to a "polyclinic," except that the medical staff members of a health center are all generalists. Although the Royal Commission on Medical Education (1968) opined that future general practice should be based almost exclusively on health centers, by March 1977 only 17% of general practitioners were working in such a setting (Dept. of Health and Social Security, 1977).

The extent, nature, and management of psychosocial disorder in British general practice have been the subjects of a series of investigations carried out over the past fifteen years by the General Practice Research Unit at the Institute of Psychiatry. One of the earliest of these investigations was a general practice morbidity survey (Shepherd et al., 1966), in which doctors from 46 London practices recorded, for a period of one year, information on all consultations with a 1/8 sample of their patients. Of some 15,000 patients at risk during the study year, more than 2,000 (approximately 14%) consulted their doctor at least once for a condition diagnosed as entirely or largely psychiatric in nature. The bulk of these patients would be classifiable in the International Classification of Diseases as suffering from neurotic or personality disorders, with psychotic conditions being much less common.

For each psychiatric case identified in the study, the doctors were asked to record the social factors that they regarded as relevant, in the sense of being implicated in either the onset, course, or severity of the patient's illness, and the responses are displayed in table 1. Although no factors were specified for a proportion of cases, it appeared that in general, the doctors regarded social factors as important in the etiology of psychiatric illness. They tended to report concurrent factors such as marital disharmony, housing problems, and work difficulties, rather than more remote influences such as childhood experiences, and there was a surprising conformity of opinion among the survey doctors as to which factors were more common and more important. Apart from "occupational and employment" problems, all the social factors were more commonly recorded for female patients, and the distribution of the factors varied considerably with age.

If a prediction had been made from these findings as to the kind of treatment most favored by the general practitioners it would surely have been that advice, counseling, and psychotherapy have at least as important a part to play as that of drugs, and that a great deal of referral to and cooperation with social agencies might be anticipated. The facts, however, argued otherwise (table 2).

The vast majority of patients received prescriptions for one or more type of drug, combined in only about a quarter of the cases

TABLE 1

Social Factors Associated with Psychiatric Illness

Social Factors	Psychotic[a] %	Neurotic[a] %	Psycho-somatic[a] %	Other[ab] %
Early environment and upbringing	3.0	2.9	1.9	1.5
Adolescent stress, engagement, pre-marital problems	–	2.3	2.1	1.0
Sexual problems	3.0	3.4	1.5	3.0
Marital problems	8.3	14.5	10.7	27.2
Child management	3.0	4.5	3.4	5.4
Dependent relatives	2.3	5.7	6.0	7.4
Housing and other domestic problems	4.5	6.8	4.1	10.4
Bereavement and widowhood	3.8	9.1	7.1	7.9
Occupational and employment	2.3	9.0	11.1	11.4
Overwork, studying, examination stress	0.8	3.8	3.0	1.0
Other factors	4.5	7.2	7.1	11.9
Number of psychiatric patients	132	1,249	466	202

[a] Percentages are not additive since in some cases more than one factor was recorded.

[b] "Other" includes patients with psychosocial problems and multiple psychiatric diagnoses.

Reprinted with permission from Shepherd et al. (1966).

with some form of superficial psychotherapy; thus, it appears that the majority of patients did not have the benefit of reassurance, counseling, or advice from their doctor. Although social factors were implicated by the doctors in over half of the 200 patients identified as suffering from psychiatric disorder, in only 27 cases was there any recorded mention of referral to or liaison with any social or welfare agency.

These findings acted as the impetus for a series of studies concerned with the nature and management of psychosocial disorder in primary care, of which three areas will be described: (1) the measurement of psychosocial disorder in the community; (2) social correlates of psychiatric disorder; and (3) general-practitioner and social-worker liaison.

TABLE 2

Treatment and Management of Psychiatric Patients

Treatment and Management	Psychotic[a] %	Neurotic[a] %	Psycho-somatic[a] %	Other[ab] %
Sedatives	18.2	32.6	26.4	26.7
Tonics and placebos	2.3	5.4	6.0	8.9
Stimulants (Amphet-amine, etc.)	4.5	6.5	2.8	4.9
Tranquilizers and/or antidepressant drugs	32.6	19.8	5.8	14.8
Reassurance, discus-sion, counseling	6.8	25.1	22.3	33.2
General practitioner psychotherapy	—	1.6	1.7	0.5
Referral to psychiatrist and/or mental hospital admission	25.0	4.8	0.6	4.9
Referral to nonpsy-chiatric consultant	6.8	2.3	6.6	9.4
Recommendation or referral to social or welfare agency	2.3	1.0	0.2	4.9
Symptomatic	6.1	7.0	25.7	20.8
"Other" or not known	0.8	0.5	0.9	1.0
No treatment recorded	34.8	27.8	27.9	22.8
Number of psychiatric patients	132	1,249	466	202

[a] Percentages add to more than 100% since in a number of cases more than one form of treatment and management was recorded.

[b] "Other" includes patients with psychosocial problems and multiple psychiatric diagnoses.

Reprinted with permission from Shepherd et al. (1966).

The Measurement of Psychosocial Disorder in the Community

Investigating the relationship between psychological and social disorder in general practice (or, for that matter, in any setting) immediately raises problems of definition and measurement of both psychiatric and social status.

The Measurement of Psychiatric Status—The measurement of psychiatric status in the community is closely related to the concept of screening for psychiatric disorder. This has been reviewed extensively by Eastwood (1971), but essentially, a two-stage model of screening has been developed: in the first stage, a large number of individuals are screened with a questionnaire designed to identify probable cases, who, in the second stage, are interviewed by a psychiatrist to confirm (or not) that the respondent does indeed have a psychiatric disorder.

Such a technique requires a valid, reliable, and economical instrument to select out the potential cases from a large population; and a standardized, reliable, and appropriate psychiatric interview schedule for use in the second stage.

Instruments for both stages of screening have been developed by the General Practice Research Unit: the General Health Questionnaire (GHQ) (Goldberg, 1972) for use in the first stage, and the Standardized Psychiatric Interview (Goldberg et al., 1970) for use in the second. The Standardized Psychiatric Interview will be described first, because it was developed first and was used in the development of the GHQ.

Standardized Psychiatric Interview—A number of reliable standardized interviews have been developed in recent years. Many of them however, are unsuitable for use in general practice and community surveys (Williams et al., 1979). Many are too time consuming to administer in a large survey, and in the main, they consist of data derived from, and are validated on, patients undergoing psychiatric treatment. This, as Dohrenwend et al. (1978) point out, leads to "a too exclusive focus on extremes of symptomatology that are rare in general populations" (p. 736). With these considerations in mind, a standardized interview was constructed especially for use in general practice and community surveys. It was designed to meet the following requirements:

1. Psychiatric assessment should be made by an experienced psychiatrist in a realistic clinical setting.
2. The interview should be acceptable to individuals who may not see themselves as psychiatrically disturbed.
3. The content of the interview should be appropriate to the types of psychiatric disturbance commonly encountered in the community.
4. The interview should generate information about individual symptoms and signs of illness as well as an overall diagnostic assessment.
5. It should discriminate clearly both between mentally disturbed and normal individuals and between patients with different degrees of psychiatric disturbance.

6. It should be relatively economical of time so that large numbers of patients can be included.
7. The psychiatric assessments and clinical ratings should be reliable in the sense of being reproducible by different trained observers. [Goldberg et al., 1970]

The schedule has four sections. The first is a relatively unstructured record of the patient's medical history, and the second part of the interview is a more detailed and systematic enquiry about any psychiatric symptoms that the patient may have experienced in the past week, and allows for ratings of ten symptom areas. The third part is again relatively unstructured and allows for the collection of as much information about the respondent's family and personal history as is thought necessary to make a clinical assessment.

The fourth part is that, at the end of the interview, the doctor makes ratings of twelve "manifest abnormalities" that he has observed at interview: there are three ratings for abnormalities of behavior, four for abnormal moods, and five for perceptual and cognitive abnormalities.

Thus, the interviewer makes in all 22 ratings, each on a 5-point scale. A rating of 0 indicates absence of a symptom; 1, a habitual trait or borderline symptom not causing distress or requiring treatment; 2, 3, and 4 respectively indicate mild, moderate, and severe degrees of a definitely mental symptom. In addition, an overall severity rating is made, again along a 5-point scale, where 0 = normal; 1 = minor abnormality stopping short of clinical significance; and 2, 3, and 4 are mild, moderate, and severe psychiatric disturbance respectively. Goldberg et al. (1970) found an interrater reliability for the reported symptoms of +0.95, and for the manifest abnormalities, +0.82.

The General Health Questionnaire—This instrument (Goldberg, 1972) was designed to identify nonpsychotic psychiatric disturbance in the community, and as such, is a measure of current emotional status rather than a diagnostic instrument or a measure of relatively stable attributes such as neuroticism. There are three versions of the questionnaire, with 12, 30, and 60 items respectively.

The items were initially derived from the clinical experience of practicing psychiatrists and from a number of previously designed questionnaires. They are concerned mainly with four areas of pathology: depression, anxiety, hypochondriasis, and social impairment. The questions and response categories were formulated to minimize the influence of personality, e.g., "have you recently been feeling sad and gloomy?" "No more than usual, rather more than usual."

The initial item pool was then administered to three groups of individuals: severely ill patients on the disturbed wards of a mental hospital; mildly ill, psychiatric outpatients; and "normals," respondents drawn from the community who were judged well on the basis of six criteria (specified in Goldberg, 1972). On the basis of this calibration study, a questionnaire of 60 items was prepared, which was then subjected to tests of reliability and validity.

The instrument was found to be acceptably reliable: Goldberg (1972) obtained split-half reliability of +0.95 and test-retest reliability of +0.90. The instrument was validated against the Clinical Interview Schedule (CIS) in a general practice setting, and yielded a misclassification rate of 8.5%, and sensitivity and specificity of 96.7 and 87.8% respectively. The instrument performed comparably well in a medical outpatient clinic, yielding values of 10.9, 80.6, and 93.3% for misclassification rate, sensitivity, and specificity respectively.

The 30-item version was similarly validated against the CIS in an American primary-care setting, and was found to perform slightly less well, yielding a misclassification rate of 19.1%, sensitivity of 85.0%, and specificity of 79.5%.

The Measurement of Social Dysfunction—As with the measurement of psychiatric disorder, the assessment of social maladjustment raises many methodological problems. Although a number of scales and inventories have been developed (Weissmann, 1975), there is still a need for an instrument that is sufficiently comprehensive to assess all the important areas of social function, yet is suitable for use in general practice and community settings, by workers with a wide range of professional backgrounds. These considerations were borne in mind in the development of the Social Assessment Schedule (Clare and Cairns, 1978).

Preliminary examination of the literature indicated a number of areas, or domains, of social behavior, which were organized within three categories (see table 3). The first category, material conditions, represents an attempt to assess objective social circumstances, and includes such areas as finance, occupation, and housing. The second category, social management, attempts to assess the individual's management of his social affairs, activities, and relationships, and includes areas such as financial management, leisure and social activities, family and domestic relationships, and marriage. The

TABLE 3

Distribution of Items Rated on the Social Schedule by Rating Category

	Rating Category with Each Item Rated Shown below the Appropriate Category: Material Conditions	Social Management	Satisfaction
Housing	Housing conditions	Household care	Housing
	Residential stability	Management of housekeeping	
Occupation/social role	Occupational stability	Quality of personal interaction with workmates	Occupation/social role (includes housewives, unemployed, disabled, retired)
	Opportunities for interaction with workmates[a]		Personal interaction
Economic situation	Family income	Management of income	Income
Leisure/social activities	Opportunities for leisure and social activities	Extent of leisure and social activities	Leisure and social activities
	Opportunities for interaction with neighbors[a]	Quality of interaction with neighbors	Interaction with neighbors
			Heterosexual role
Family and domestic relationships	Opportunities for interaction with relatives[a]	Quality of interaction with relatives	Interaction with relatives
		Quality of solitary living	Solitary living
	Opportunities for domestic interaction (i.e., with unrelated others or adult offspring in household)	Quality of domestic interaction (i.e., with unrelated others or adult offspring in household)	Domestic interaction

	Situational handicaps to child management[a]	Child management	Parental role
		Fertility and family planning	
Marital		Sharing of responsibilities and decision making	Marital harmony
		Sharing of interests and activities	Sexual compatability

[a]This group of items rates objective restrictions which might be expected to impair functioning in the appropriate area. "Situational handicaps to child management" assesses difficulties likely to exacerbate normal problems of child-rearing, e.g., inadequate living space, an absent parent. Objective restrictions on leisure activities include extreme age, physical disabilities, heavy domestic or work commitments, isolated situation of the home, etc.

Reprinted with permission from Clare and Cairns (1978).

third category, satisfaction, is composed of ratings intended to be a measure of the respondent's attitude toward various aspects of his life situation, e.g., housing, marital relationships.

Thus, the schedule examines each individual's life from three main standpoints: what he has, what he does with it, and how he feels about it. These three categories are intended to be operationally independent, and wherever possible, each aspect of social adjustment receives a rating for each category. Rating of items are made using a 4-point scale, ranging from 0 (satisfactory; no difficulties; satisfied) to 3 (severe difficulties; severe dissatisfaction). Thus the scale is essentially negative, measuring degrees of dysfunction and maladjustment, with no attempts at measuring different degrees of satisfactory functioning. A number of studies have shown the interrater reliability of this schedule to be extremely high (Clare and Cairns, 1978).

Social Correlates of Psychiatric Disorder

The 1966 morbidity survey indicated that substantial social morbidity was associated with psychiatric disorder in general practice, but the measurement of social morbidity was entirely subjective, i.e., the general practitioner's opinion. With the development of the social interview schedule, it was possible to investigate this association more objectively.

Sylph et al. (1969) and Cooper (1972) described a study that had two aims: to test the hypothesis that clinically identified neurotic patients (in the community) were characterized by impaired social functioning, and to examine the nature of any characteristic social difficulties.

To these ends, a case-control study was carried out using patients from eight general practices in South London. The index cases were selected from among those given a psychiatric diagnosis by the general practitioner, and in whom the duration of illness exceeded one year. Control patients were selected from the clinic attenders with no known psychiatric symptoms, and individual pairs were matched for sex, age, marital status, occupational status, and social class. Patients thus selected were given the standardized psychiatric interview, and any index patient not confirmed as psychiatric and any control patient found to have significant psychiatric symptoms were rejected. Eighty-one matched pairs were thus generated, and each patient was seen individually at home and given the standardized social interview.

Anxiety neurosis and depressive neurosis together were found to account for 80% of the patients: accordingly, anxiety and depression, with their concomitants of insomnia, fatigue, irritability, and loss of concentration, were the most commonly observed abnormalities at clinical interview. With regard to the social interview scores, the number of 0 ratings ("satisfactory") was higher for both sexes in the control group, and conversely, ratings of 2 and 3, indicating serious dysfunction, were much more frequent in the index group. Figure 1 shows the mean area scores for the two groups of patients, indicating that the intergroup differences extended across all areas of social functioning. However, when the ratings were grouped into the three broad categories of material conditions, social management, and role satisfaction, the differences were greater for the two latter categories than for the first. A separate analysis of the relationship between clinical and social ratings for 115 chronic

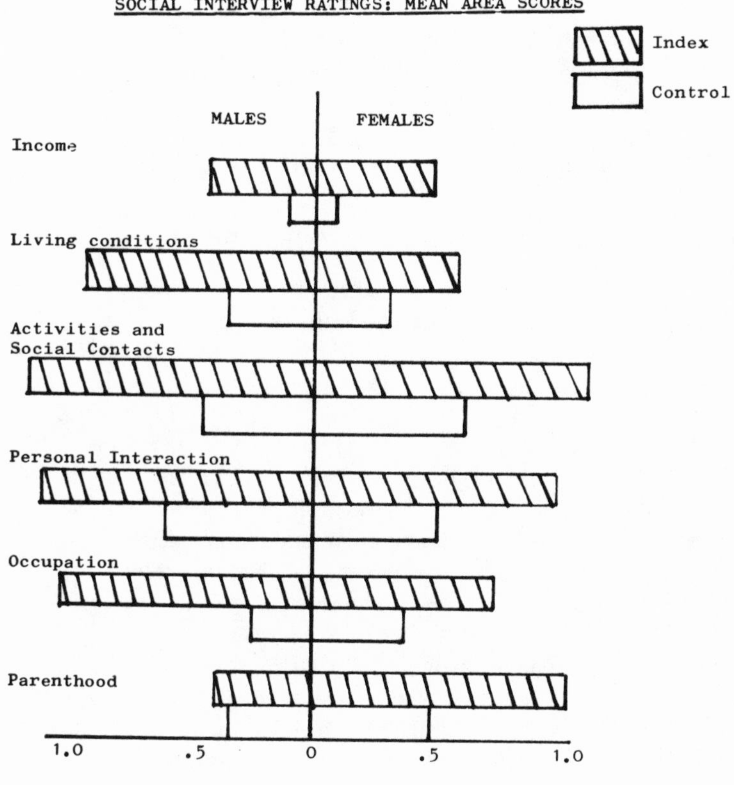

From Cooper (1972)

neurotic patients (including the 81 in the case-control study) yielded significant positive correlations between clinical severity scores and social management (+0.37) and role satisfaction (+0.32), but not for material conditions (+0.13, n.s.).

While the presence of social problems among psychiatric patients does not inevitably imply that social welfare agencies should be mobilized in every case, the detailed examination and treatment of social problems is often time consuming and complex, and may require skills tangential to those acquired during medical training. Even general practitioners whose view of their role is essentially holistic often find themselves unable to devote as much time as they would wish to the social aspects of illness, and thus the effective management of a significant proportion of patients such as those described above will inevitably involve a social agency of some kind.

In a pilot study (Sylph et al., 1969) carried out with the first 20 of the 81 matched pairs referred to above, the research team reexamined each index case, to determine whether, in their opinion, social intervention was appropriate. In 12 out of the 20, social intervention was thought likely to have been beneficial, and in half of these, such intervention was thought to be urgent.

Findings such as these prompt further investigation of the liaison between general practitioners and social work services.

General-Practitioner and Social-Worker Liaison

Although they are both the responsibility of the same government department (the Department of Health and Social Security), the general medical services and the personal social services in the United Kingdom are administered quite separately. While general practitioners are part of the National Health Service, the social services are administered by the local authorities, and prior to 1970 were the responsibility of the Medical Officer of Health. The Committee of Local Authority and Allied Personal Social Services (the "Seebohm Report," 1968) recommended that each local authority should set up a Social Services Department, responsible to a Director of Social Services, and this recommendation became a requirement of the Local Authority Social Services Act 1970. Thus, a typical social services department, under its director, consists of a number of "area intake teams" of social workers, situated in local area offices, as well as a number of specialist social-worker teams to deal with special groups of clients, e.g., the elderly, the physically handicapped, etc.

The Seebohm report emphasized the need for liason between the general medical and the social services: "We regard teamwork between general practitioners and social workers as vital. It is one of our main objectives and the likelihood of promoting it is a test we would like to see applied to our proposals for a social services department" (p. 215).

The Seebohm committee, however, recognized the contemporary lack of liaison between general practitioners and social workers. This was one of the findings of the 1966 prevalence survey (Shepherd et al., 1966), and was confirmed by Harwin et al. (1970) who interviewed all the general practitioners in the London Borough of Croydon (N = 123) with regard to their experience of and attitudes toward social workers. Only 5% reported regular or frequent contact with social workers, while for the great majority, contact was infrequent and invariably initiated by the social workers. The two professions were seldom in communication, and meetings (as opposed to telephone contacts) tended to relate to urgent hospital admission rather than to problems of community care. The doctors were also asked about experience of other statutory social agencies, (e.g., probation officers, child-care officers) and contact with voluntary agencies (e.g., Alcoholics Anonymous). About two-thirds of the survey doctors could recall no contact with a probation officer or child-care officer about any of their patients, and about 80% of the practitioners had no contact with local voluntary agencies, and indeed, were often unaware of their existence

This dearth of contact with social workers might be regarded as an expression of hostility on the part of the general practitioners. An examination of their attitudes revealed that while a minority voiced criticism, the majority had no views on the local social services because their acquaintance with them was so scanty, and it became clear that most of the practitioners had never given serious thought to the possibility of collaborating with social workers.

This state of affairs was further confirmed by a national survey of Directors of Social Services (Ratoff et al., 1973). Although the Seebohm committee had recommended that social workers be specifically attached to general practitioners, only 1.5% of social workers in Great Britain were deployed in this way.

Findings such as these acted as the impetus for the establishment of an experimental social-work attachment scheme in Croydon. Initially, one social worker was attached to one group practice of four doctors (Cooper et al., 1974), but the "attachment scheme" has since expanded so that at present (1979) four social workers are attached to four practices; three of the practices (9 doctors) work from a health center, and the other (2 doctors) from private premises a few miles distant. The social workers spend approximately two-thirds of their time working with the general practitioners, taking referrals (both short- and long-term) from them and other members of the primary care team, and are directly involved in feedback and case discussion.

This experimental scheme has been the subject of both observational and experimental studies.

Observational Studies in the Social-Work Attachment Scheme

Corney and Briscoe (1977) and Corney and Bowen (1980) monitored the pattern of referrals to the "attached" social workers, and compared this with referrals to the local authority social services department. Corney and Briscoe (1977), in a preliminary study, compared data from the first 300 referrals to the attachment scheme with data collected by Rickards et al. (1976) from clients referred to the intake teams of Croydon borough. They found that the two client populations were similar in terms of sex, age, and the proportion suffering from physical ill health, but that the proportion of psychiatric morbidity (as identified by the social worker) was higher in the attachment-scheme clients than in the local-authority clients, and that they were more likely to need casework than practical measures.

This study had several shortcomings, however. The data from the two settings were collected over different periods of time, and the information was limited in scope. Also, the attachment scheme had only just started, and thus an atypical clientele may have been referred. Thus, Corney and Bowen (1980) compared all referrals to the attachment scheme and the local authority intake team over a period of three months.

During that time, 82 cases were referred to the attached social workers and 119 to the intake team: very few clients in the latter group were referred by general practitioners. Although both groups continued a preponderance of females, this was especially marked for the attachment group, probably reflecting the higher female attendance at the health center. With regard to age, the attachment group contained a higher proportion of clients under 44 years and a lower proportion over 65 years than the intake group. The distribution of marital status was similar for both groups.

The social workers were asked to record the reasons why the client was referred, using a scheme modified from Fitzgerald (1978). Table 4 shows that a higher proportion of intake clients were referred with practical and material problems, whereas the attach-

TABLE 4
Reasons for Referral

Reasons	Intake N	Intake %	Attachment N	Attachment %
Material/practical problems				
Housing	18	15.1	8	9.8
Financial	23	19.3	9	11.0
Other practical problems	5	4.2	2	2.4
Subtotal	46	38.6	19	23.2
Relationship, emotional problems & minor mental ill health				
Marital	8	6.7	13	15.9
Child & family care	11	9.2	8	9.8
Social isolation/bereavement	1	0.8	6	7.3
Emotional problem/mental illness in client or family	9	7.7	15	18.3
Other problems	11	9.2	4	4.8
Subtotal	40	33.6	46	56.1
Problems associated with physical disability				
Home management in the elderly	20	16.8	11	13.4
Physical disability/ill health	7	5.9	4	4.9
Subtotal	27	22.7	15	18.3
Other problems	6	5.0	2	2.4
Total	119	100.0	82	100.0

Adapted with permission from Corney and Bowen (1980).

ment group contained more clients referred for relationship and emotional problems. These differences occurred mainly in clients under 65 years; in the elderly, the reasons for referral to both facilities were similar.

The social workers were also asked to record any medical diagnosis mentioned by the referring agent. The two groups continued similar proportions of individuals with physical diagnoses, but there were marked differences with regard to mental ill health. About 45% of the attachment group had a psychiatric diagnosis recorded (mainly minor mental illness) compared with about 15% of the intake group.

These differences reflect in part the attachment social worker's closer relationship with the referring agent (i.e., the general practitioner), as well as any real difference in the clientele. Thus, the social workers were also asked to record their own assessment of the client's major problems. Table 5 indicates that, although there were still differences between the two groups, a high proportion of clients in both groups had problems in more than one area.

The two types of social worker differ also in the intensity of client contact. Corney (1980), using data from the same cohorts of clients, monitored the intensity of client-social worker contact, and the principal findings from this study are summarized in table 6. The social workers attached to the general practitioners interviewed their clients more often and were in touch with them for a longer period of time than the local-authority intake social workers. These differences applied to all age groups, but were particularly marked for clients rereferred for relationship and emotional problems.

In this study, no information was obtained on outcome of social workers' interventions, and it is therefore not known whether the greater intensity of contact is any more helpful. However, a preliminary inspection of the results of an unpublished study (R.H. Corney, personal communication) of clients' opinions indicates that while an approximately equal proportion of clients in both groups regarded themselves as "satisfied" with the help that they received, a greater proportion of the attachment-scheme clients regarded themselves as having been helped.

Experimental Studies of Social-Work Involvement

Cooper et al. (1975) compared the outcome of chronic neurotic

TABLE 5

Social Workers Assessments of Their Clients' Problems

Problems	Intake N	Intake %	Attachment N	Attachment %
Relationship/emotional/mental illness	20	16.8	23	28.0
Practical	22	18.5	3	3.7
Physical disability/illness	17	14.3	4	4.8
Relationship & practical	26	21.8	25	30.5
Relationship & physical disability	7	5.9	8	9.8
Practical & physical disability	17	14.3	11	13.4
Relationship, practical & physical disability	8	6.7	8	9.8
Not Known	2	1.7	0	0
Total	119	100.0	82	100.0

Adapted with permission from Corney and Bowen (1980).

TABLE 6

Intensity of Contact with Social Workers

Contacts	Intake Clients (N = 119) %	Attachment Clients (N = 82) %
Referred by phone or letter only	60	15
Length of contact with client		
$<$ 1 week	47	27
$>$ 3 months	12	38
Number of interviews		
1 only	46	23
6 or more	2	18

patients who were and were not referred to a social worker attached to a general practice (GP), essentially a comparison between usual GP treatment (the control group) and usual GP treatment plus social-work intervention (the experimental group). Ninety-two experimental patients and ninety-seven control patients were selected from among those given a diagnosis of chronic neurosis by the GP, and confirmed by standard psychiatric interview. The social adjustment of each patient was measured by the standardized social interview, and both interviews were repeated one year later. In the interim, both groups of patients received medication from their doctors as usual, and could be referred to specialist agencies in the normal way. In addition, the patients in the experimental group were seen and treated by the attached social worker.

At inception, the two groups were broadly comparable with regard to demographic variables, psychological and physical health, and social adjustment scores. During the study year, 5.4% of the experimental group and 15.5% of the control group were referred to psychiatric services, and 30 and 40% of experimental and control patients respectively were referred to outside social agencies. Thus, the findings suggest that patients and practitioners alike came to rely on the social-work service as a partial alternative to specialist agencies.

Table 7 shows the change in psychiatric and social adjustment scores. Although the psychiatric status of both groups improved over the year, the improvement was significantly greater for the experimental group. This change corresponded to changes in the patients' clinical condition. At follow-up 38% of the experimental

TABLE 7

Change of Psychiatric and Social Adjustment Ratings in Follow-up Year: Experimental and Control Groups

	Experimental Group (N = 92)	Control Group (N = 97)	Test of Significance
Psychiatric mean score			
Initially	26.9	26.1	
At follow-up	16.6	19.7	
Change in score			
Mean	−10.3	−6.4	t = 2.68
SD	10.2	9.9	P 0.01
Social adjustment mean score			
Initially	15.4	15.3	
At follow-up	12.1	15.1	
Change is score			
Mean	−3.3	−0.2	t = 4.79
SD	5.0	3.7	P 0.001

Reprinted with permission from Cooper et al. (1975).

group had been taken off psychotropic drugs and 40% were judged to be no longer in need of medical care, as compared with 25 and 23% respectively of the control group. Social scores fell appreciably for the experimental group only (table 7), the control group showing little apparent change in social adaptation during the year. These changes in the experimental group were apparent for all three major categories of social adjustment (material conditions, management, and role satisfaction), but the change was less marked for material conditions than for the other two categories. A similar study, but with relation to acutely depressed patients, is in progress.

The work which has been summarized above represents part of an ongoing program of research which has been designed to examine both theoretical and practical issues in the field of psychosocial epidemiology. Now that primary health care has become a topic of major interest throughout the world, including the United States, it is apparent that the findings reported from the United Kingdom are not atypical. The structure of the British National Health service has facilitated scientific investigation by virtue of the well-organized corps of general practitioners who constitute by far the largest single group of physicians. The implications of the findings, however, extend beyond national boundaries. Their significance has been explicitly acknowledged by a WHO report based on the experience of 12 European countries: "The crucial question is not how the general practitioner can fit into the mental health services but rather how the psychiatrist can collaborate most effectively with primary medical services and reinforce the effectiveness of the primary physician as a member of the mental health team. The primary medical care team is the keystone of community psychiatry" (WHO, 1973, p. 27).

References

Clare, A.W. & Cairns, V. (1978), Design, development and use of a standardised interview to assess social maladjustment. *Psychol. Med.*, 8:589–604.

Committee on Local Authority and Allied Personal Social Services (Seebohm Report) (1968), *Cmmd. 3703*, H.M.S.O. London.

Cooper, B. (1972), Clinical and social aspects of chronic neurosis. *Proc. Royal Soc. Med.*, 65:509–512.

Cooper, B., Harwin, B.G., Depla, C., & Shepherd, M. (1974), An experiment in community health care. *Lancet*, 2:1356–1358.

Cooper, B., & Harwin, B.G. (1975), Mental health care in the community: an evaluative study. *Psychol. Med.*, 5:372–380.

Corney, R.H. (1980), Factors affecting the operation and success of social work attachment schemes to general practice. *J. Royal Coll. Gen. Pract.*, 30:149–158.

Corney, R.H. & Bowen, B. (1980), Referrals to social workers: a comparative study of a local authority intake team with a general practice attachment scheme. *J. Royal Coll. Gen. Pract.*, 30:139–147.

Corney, R.H. & Briscoe, M.E. (1977), Social workers and their clients: a comparison between primary health care and local authority settings. *J. Royal Coll. Gen. Pract.*, 27:295–301.

Department of Health and Social Security (1977), *Annual Report*, H.M.S.O., London.

Dohrenwend, B.P., Yager, T.J., Egri, G., & Mendelsohn, F.S. (1978), The Psychiatric States Schedule as a measure of dimensions of psychopathology in the general population. *Arch. Gen. Psychiat.*, 35:731–737.

Eastwood, M.R. (1971), Screening for psychiatric disorder. *Psychol. Med.*, 1:197–208.

Fitzgerald, M. (1978), The classification and recording of social problems. *Soc. Sci. Med.*, 12:255–263.

Goldberg, D.P. (1972), *The Detection of Psychiatric Illness by Questionnaire.* London: Oxford University Press.

Goldberg, D.P., Cooper, B., Eastwood, M.R., Kedward, H.B., & Shepherd, M. (1970), A standardised interview for use in community surveys. *Brit. J. Prevent. Soc. Med.*, 24:18–23.

Harwin, B.G., Cooper, B., Eastwood, M.R., & Goldberg, D.P. (1970), Prospects for social work in general practice. *Lancet*, 2:559–561.

Hicks, D. (1976), *Primary Health Care.* London: Department of Health and Social Security.

Querido, A. (1962), Mental health programmes with public health planning. *Ment. Hyg.*, 46:626–654.

Ratoff, L., Cooper, B., & Rocket, D. (1973), Seebohm and the N.H.S.: survey of medico-social liaison. *Brit. Med. J.*, 2:51–53.

Rickards, C., Gildersleeve, C., Fitzgerald, R., & Cooper, B. (1976), The health of clients of a social services department. *J. Royal Coll. Gen. Pract.*, 26:237–243.

Royal Commission on Medical Education (Todd Report) (1968), H.M.S.O., London.

Shepherd, M., Cooper, B., Brown, A.C., & Kalton, G. (1966), *Psychiatric Illness in General Practice.* London: Oxford University Press.

Sylph, J., Kedward, H.B., & Eastwood, M.R. (1969), Chronic neurotic patients in general practice: a pilot study. *J. Royal Coll. Gen. Pract.*, 17:162–170.

Weissmann, M. (1975), The assessment of social adjustment. *Arch. Gen. Psychiat.*, 32:357–365.

Williams, P., Tarnopolsky, A., & Hand, D. (1979), Case definition and case identification in psychiatric epidemiology: review and assessment. *Psychol. Med.*, 10:101–114.

World Health Organization (1973), *Psychiatry and Primary Medical Care.* Copenhagen: WHO.

Help-Seeking in Severe Mental Illness

JOHN A. CLAUSEN

NANCY G. PFEFFER

CAROL L. HUFFINE

Hospitalization for severe mental illness is now arranged on a voluntary basis far more often than was the case a few decades ago, though the word "voluntary" cannot be construed to mean that hospitalization is the patient's first choice for dealing with his problem. But then, *general* medical patients who are hospitalized may not necessarily be enthusiastic about their physician's decision that they should be in the hospital. Mechanic (1968) has suggested that analyzing response to symptoms of mental disorder entails taking into account the same general factors that are relevant in the case of physical illness. It is true that persons other than the patient may be more centrally involved in seeking help for the patient's mental disorder. But symptoms must be recognized and interpreted in terms of their threat to the well-being of the individual and to those with whom the individual interacts, and potential sources of help must be evaluated in terms of the perceived consequences of actions that might be taken.

Such recognition and response take place in the context of established expectations and relationships that are often sharply disrupted in the case of mental disorder, and the process of definition and response to an initial episode of mental illness may entail more barriers and discontinuities than is usual in instances of physical illness (Clausen and Yarrow, 1955). What of subsequent response and help-seeking when symptoms of mental disorder recur? Does the patient with persistent symptoms come to seek psychiatric care at times of great distress? For the less persistently symptomatic former patient, can we discern any patterns in the way that subsequent episodes of distress are responded to? What elements in the situation seem to make a difference?

There have been numerous studies of the mental patient in the community and of the circumstances associated with the patient's return to the hospital. But they have not, for the most part, examined the process of help-seeking or the long-term history of use of various types of care by patient and family. Perhaps the major generalizations drawn from such research are that patients tend to be rehospitalized if they have persistent or severe symptoms (Freeman and Simmons, 1963; Angrist et al., 1968; Myers and Bean, 1968), if members of the family are emotionally involved in a critical, disapproving way—at least for schizophrenic patients (Brown et al., 1972)—and if the family has a low tolerance for the uncertainties and anxieties engendered by symptomatic behaviors (Greenley, 1979). The best predictor of rehospitalization is the number of previous admissions to a mental hospital, which may reflect family attitudes engendered by many previous admissions as well as the severity of the illness or behavior problems experienced by the patient.

Having conducted a long-term follow-up of a group of families studied previously, with specific focus on the process of the initial recognition and definition of mental illness, we now have data that may shed some additional light on the topic of longer-term help-seeking. We here examine the course of help-seeking from the initial recognition of an emotional problem (which led ultimately to hospitalization in the 1950s) over the next 15–20 years for a cohort of 80 married patients who were followed up in the early 1970s. We shall also draw upon data from a roughly comparable cohort of 39 patients who first entered treatment in the 1970s. For the group hospitalized in the 1950s, our data on help-seeking came from the spouses, who were interviewed during the period of the patient's initial hospitalization and up to six months thereafter. Follow-up data were also secured from the spouses, except in those instances where the marriage had been dissolved and the patient or another family member provided data. Interview data were obtained for approximately 80% of the patients and some record data were secured for all but five others. In the group of families and patients seen most recently, four interviews were sought with the spouse and two with the patient during the period following the patient's admission to the hospital and through six months after the patient's release from the hospital.

Study of the Initial Hospitalization

The criteria for inclusion in the research in both periods were specified in terms of the following patient characteristics: no previous hospitalization for mental disorder; a diagnosis of schizophrenia or affective psychosis, psychoneurosis, or character disorder; married and living with spouse at the time of developing symptoms; aged 20–50; white, and a legal resident of a specified community served by the hospitals included in the research. In the 1950s, three public mental hospitals serving Washington, D.C., and suburban Maryland, and one serving the San Francisco Bay Area of California were included. The East Coast sample overlaps that reported by Clausen and Yarrow (1955), excluding patients who did not meet the sampling specifications just mentioned and adding 44 families less intensively but more systematically studied in a later phase of the same project. The California families were the 17 studied by Sampson, Messinger, and Towne (1964), who made available their original data and suggested inclusion of their families in our follow-up.

The patients who entered treatment in the 1970s were drawn largely from private psychiatric facilities, though a few came from the same public mental hospitals in Maryland. It had been intended that the 1970s sample would include both a group of patients drawn from the same state mental hospitals and a group of patients now using other types of facilities, largely outpatient. Monitoring intake at the various state hospitals revealed, however, that very few married patients were being admitted with a diagnosis of functional psychoses or psychoneurosis unless they had previously been treated in other facilities. Moreover, monitoring outpatient facilities in the counties under consideration revealed that severely disturbed patients who had not previously been hospitalized tended to be referred to inpatient facilities, most often small private hospitals or the psychiatric wards of general hospitals. We therefore decided to select patients from a number of such facilities to which referrals were made by the various services monitored. Since a major interest of our research was in tracing the process of recognition and definition of mental disorder, it was imperative that the patients not have experienced prior episodes of treated disorder.

The sample of patients and families who first confronted mental illness in the past decade is somewhat older, married longer, and of higher social status than the patients and families seen 20 years earlier. Male patients in the two cohorts are reasonably similar in age and social status, but female patients in the 1970s group are, on the average, about eight years older and significantly more likely to be from middle-class backgrounds (71 versus 35%). In each group, however, patients were an unselected segment of successive admissions—that is, unselected by any criterion other than willingness of the spouse (and in the new cohort, of the patient) to participate in the research. The great majority of spouses and more than half of the patients approached agreed to participate.

Although our research was not specifically focused on help-seeking behavior, the initial interviews with spouses in all instances (and with patients in those instances where the patient was interviewed) sought information on the nature of the mental-health problem as originally perceived and on the course of efforts to deal with that problem. Attitudes toward the various types of health services used were secured during the course of the initial episode of treatment and in its immediate aftermath. The follow-up of families of the patients whose initial hospitalization took place in the 1950s inquired also into subsequent episodes of symptomatic behavior, treatment received, and modes of coping in the families.

Recognition and Response to Initial Symptoms—In earlier reports of the research, we noted that the great majority of husbands and wives did not recognize the initial manifestations of acute, serious mental disorder (Yarrow et al., 1955). The patients most common symptoms, reported when the spouse realized something was wrong, were being nervous, upset, and irritable. Such behavior was reported by roughly four-fifths of the spouses in both the 1950s and the 1970s groups. From one-fourth to one-half of the patients were described as having serious delusions or hallucinations in the early period of symptoms, but these were frequently interpreted as merely a reflection of being upset.

Husbands and wives tended to interpret the initial manifestations of psychosis or severe neurosis in the framework of interpersonal tensions in the marriage or to attribute the problem to personality or character weakness in the patient, to stress, or to physical illness more often than to emotional causes. The prevalent response was to wait and see what might develop, even among those spouses who suspected an emotional problem or who attributed the problem to physical causes, though a few suggested seeing the family physician.

Roughly one-fourth of the patients in both cohorts at some point prior to admission to the hospital expressed the fear that they might be mentally ill, but generally such expressions were cancelled out by alternative explanations of their distress. Female patients who expressed fear that they might be mentally ill were somewhat more likely than male patients to request help. Several male patients sought help when they were aware of strong impulses to harm their wives. In these instances the wives were uniformly skeptical that there was any need for psychiatric help.

The spouse's response to the patient's discomfort and agitation tended to be suffused with annoyance, anger, and feelings of extreme confusion. Interpersonal tensions were greatest in families where the marital relationship had already been seriously strained—roughly three-fifths of the families with a female patient and somewhat less than a third when the patient was a male. The spouse was predominantly sympathetic primarily in families where the marital relationship had been good.

In general, there was very little communication between husband and wife, or it was characterized by increased argument and conflict. In the relatively few cases (roughly one-fourth of the families) where relevant communication about the patient's problem took place, it did not tend to lead to earlier consultation with a physician or to seeking psychiatric care. Often these couples sought an explanation for the patient's upset in stressful events or in difficult circumstances and they expected that the upset would subside. Hospitalization was seldom considered more than a month before it occurred even when the symptomatic behaviors were extremely bizarre.

Fear of Stigmatization—To what extent does fear of stigmatization prevent either the patient or the spouse from seeking psychiatric help? We cannot answer this question directly, but if we use restricted communication to friends and neighbors regarding the patient's hospitalization as an index of fear of stigmatization, we can compare those husbands and wives who restrict communication with those who communicate freely. In our original 1950s sample, roughly one-third of the spouses were relatively frank in letting others know about the patient's hospitalization. Communication was more open in the 1970s sample; very few spouses now attempt to conceal completely the fact of psychiatric hospitalization, but one-third report that they restrict communication to relatives and close friends. We may assume that these are the spouses who feel a sense of stigma and we shall so refer to them.

In our 1970s sample, spouses who apparently feared stigmatization were less likely to interpret the patient's original problematic behavior as evidence of mental disorder. Wives who had a sense of stigma most often interpreted the husband's behavior as evidence of being upset; none of the six wives in this group entertained the possibility of mental disorder in the early stages, most ascribing the problematic behavior to their husband's being "upset." By contrast, two-fifths of the wives who did not have a sense of stigma made an early interpretation of mental disorder and none referred to their husbands as being "upset." In the case of husbands of female patients, those with a sense of stigma more often made the interpretation of a physical problem; none made a mental-illness interpretation.

There was no difference in the average time at which help was sought between those who appeared to fear stigmatization and those who were free in their communication about the patient's hospitalization. There was a significant difference, however, in the locus of control of the decision to hospitalize: medical and other authorities were involved far more often in the case of patients whose spouses feared stigmatization. Moreover, those who felt a sense of stigma were substantially more likely to report subsequently that they had reservations as to whether the patient's hospitalization had been the right decision. Such reservations were most frequent among wives of male patients who feared stigma as contrasted with those who did not ($p < 0.01$).

Unfortunately, we have less-adequate data on the effects of feelings of stigma in the original study and our findings are less strong, though generally consonant with the later data. One finding that comes through clearly in both cohorts is that spouses who restrict communication about the patient's hospitalization are significantly more likely to be coded as having responded to the patient's problem with sympathy. They also had perceived the patient's personality more positively in the period prior to symptoms of severe distress. It appears that a positive perception, coupled with sympathy, makes the threat of mental disorder more difficult to entertain. Thus we may not be dealing with the direct effects of stigma so much as with the meaning of communicating information that might be seen as discrediting a loved one.

General Medical Consultations—At some point after the recognition of a problem, about two-thirds of the patients went to see a physician. Slightly more than half of those who consulted a physician saw him alone, though often only after they had been strongly urged to do so by their spouses. Most of the other patients who consulted a physician either went with their spouses or received a home visit which permitted communication between the physician and both spouses. Joint consultations, especially in the case of male patients, led to psychiatric referrals and to relatively quick hospitalization far more frequently then did a patient's solo visit. Whereas nearly three-fourths of the male patients who initially went to the family physician alone did so more than six months before admission, 85% of the patients who went with their wives or received a home visit were hospitalized within one month after the initial contact with the physician. The same tendency is found for female patients, though the differences are not so striking.

Is the explanation to be found in the presentation of symptoms? Not for men, at least. Male patients who went with their wives actually exhibited somewhat less extreme or bizarre symptoms than did those who made solo visits to the physician in the early stages of their difficulty. In the case of female patients, however, the husband and wife went together to the family physician primarily in those instances where the patient manifested bizarre symptoms or significant delusions. Female patients were, nevertheless, much more likely to be given palliative treatment by the general physician and less likely to receive a psychiatric referral in the early stages of the symptomatic behavior.

The greater likelihood of a psychiatric referral in instances of joint consultation by husband and wife with the physician would seem to derive at least in part from the communication by the spouse of problematic behaviors that the patient would be unlikely to report. For example, one wife reported that when her husband dwelt on his physical malaise, she brought to the physician's attention her husband's panic the night before for fear that he would die of a disease he clearly did not have. Also, seeing a man accompanied by his wife may be sufficiently unusual to lead a physician to consider its psychological implications.

Voluntary Versus Committed Patients—Women were more likely to have been committed on index admission than were men, and this was true for groups matched on sociodemographic characteristics and diagnosis. Two-thirds of the women in our original sample were initially committed versus slightly less than half the men, and an additional one in six of the women was committed after admission. None of the seven men who were hospitalized for psychoneurosis or character disorder was committed, but several women diagnosed as psychoneurotic were committed.

Men who were committed tended to enter the hospital after relatively brief periods of problematic behavior, while the opposite was true of women who were committed. Almost all of the women whose onset was seen as gradual and who had long been symptomatic were committed, either by their husbands or by authorities to whom their husbands turned.

Men who expressed fear that they might have a mental illness tended to enter the hospital on a voluntary basis, but eight out of 10 women who made such an interpretation were either committed at admission or shortly thereafter. While diagnosis and the nature of symptoms presented were both related to admission status, the nature of the husband-wife relationship, and the communication patterns between husband and wife had even greater influence on the action taken. From the entire transcript of the interview with the spouse, we coded whether the spouse was primarily oriented to the patient's needs or to his or her own needs, whether the basic response to the patient's distress was sympathetic or not, and whether there was substantial two-way communication between patient and spouse in the period just prior to admission. Spouses oriented primarily toward the patient's needs were more likely to persuade the patient to enter the hospital voluntarily, and the same was true of the highly overlapping group of spouses who responded sympathetically to the patient's distress. Close communication (as contrasted with mutual withdrawal or hostile bickering) was associated both with sympathetic response and high levels of voluntary admission for both sexes, though as noted earlier, it did not affect the timing of seeking professional help.

Husbands who reported that they had been annoyed, angry, and confused as a result of their wives' mental disorder overwhelmingly committed their wives. Commitment was a way of resolving long-standing tensions that derived at least in part from many months of symptomatic behavior. Wives of male patients, on the other hand, were most likely to undertake commitment if they were *afraid* of their symptomatic husbands; in such instances, eight of eight (six of whom were diagnosed as having manic-depressive psychosis) undertook commitment proceedings.

Thus, our findings indicate marked sex differences in sensitivity to the spouse's behavior, in attempts at sympathetic understanding, and in the use of power during the initial period of the patient's distress. Both patient and spouse interviews, in both cohorts, suggest that wives of male patients are more aware of the patient's moods and needs and are more supportive. In part we attribute this to a real difference in the interpersonal sensitivity of women and men characteristic of American society. In part it may also reflect the nature of male selection where psychologically vulnerable (especially schizophrenic) persons are involved. We shall have more to say on this point later.

The Patient's Perspective—Commitment was much less frequent among more recently hospitalized patients, but the reports of the patients themselves as well as those of their spouses corroborate the greater tendency for husbands to be dominant in the decision to hospitalize female patients. Whereas a fifth of the male patients said that they alone had made the decision to enter a mental hospital, almost none of the female patients felt that the decision had been predominantly theirs. Many had acceded to pressure to enter the hospital as voluntary patients, though nearly a fifth of the women reported no recall of the events leading up to hospitalization.

More than half of the patients were unwilling to refer to their episode of acute psychological distress (most often entailing markedly bizarre behavior) as reflective of "mental illness." Even those who did use the term or its more acceptable popular equivalent, "nervous breakdown," frequently went on to explain their behaviors during the episode in terms that attentuated symptoms or normalized their acts. Less than one-sixth reported on the events preceding hospitalization in a realistic or insightful way. In discussing their earlier symptoms and behaviors, there was a tendency for the former patient to be selective, focusing on what precipitated distress or giving a highly generalized or intellectualized account of events that had been nightmarish for their spouses. For example, a professional who had been totally out of contact and incoherent at hospitalization reported: "I wasn't communicating well," a nice attenuation of the symptoms presented. He also reported, however, that the day before he entered the hospital, he had called a physician friend and "asked him if I was showing signs of psychosis." His friend told him that he was indeed showing such symptoms, but this did not lead him to seek treatment directly. His wife was attempting to arrange a psychiatric consultation when he became completely unmanageable and had to be taken to the hospital by the police.

During the period between the onset of symptoms and the final resolution by hospitalization of these patients, many tried to cope with their tensions in various ways. Roughly half of the prepatients report that they tried changing life routines or taking other action to relieve tensions. These ranged from vacations to heavier investment in work or in religion on the part of men. Women employed for pay more often gave up their jobs. Beyond this, half of the male patients acknowledged a substantial increase in alcohol consumption, often to the point of impairing their functioning, and another fourth of the men took tranquilizers, often prescribed by the family physician. None of the women acknowledged heavier drinking but two-thirds said that they turned to tranquilizers to relieve tension.

Active help-seeking is more likely to be initiated by the spouse than by anyone else, as reported in our earlier publications (Clausen and Yarrow, 1955). But closer analysis of more detailed data reveals that cues from others were often highly influential. In instances of relatively early hospitalization, for example, more than half the spouses reported that others—friends, co-workers of the patient, or relatives—had commented on the patient's problematic behavior and sometimes suggested the need for action.

We have elsewhere reported on the difficulties encountered by families in trying to determine how to deal with the problem even after it has been recognized as being a mental disorder (Clausen and Yarrow, 1955). It is gratifying to be able to report that there seem to be far fewer difficulties of this sort in the 1970s than were in the 1950s. Most physicians seem better informed about existing facilities for the care of mental disorder, and of course there are many more such facilities. But the process of defining the initial symptoms and of coming to a decision to seek psychiatric care is not markedly different in the 1970s from what it was in the 1950s. Uncertainties and interpersonal tensions, as well as processes of normalization and attenuation of the patient's problematic behaviors still make the course of help-seeking long and arduous. Moreover, it appears that considerations of social control weigh more heavily in the help-seeking process than do considerations of therapy within an illness frame of reference.

Help-Seeking and Treatment in the Early Posthospital Period

Data were secured in the 1950s from about half of the members of the original study group relating to their status in the first six months after release from the hospital. Roughly two-thirds of the spouses had favored further treatment following hospitalization, but only one-third of the patients actually entered treatment of any sort, most often outpatient treatment linked to the hospital. For those who did so, a fourth of the spouses reported that treatment had been very helpful but a slightly larger proportion reported no appreciable effect or even a negative effect. One patient in ten was rehospitalized in the first six months. Very few of the spouses of men and women hospitalized in the 1950s had more than cursory contact with the patient's therapist, and to our knowledge there were no instances of cotherapy of husband and wife in the period immediately following hospitalization.

The early posthospital experience of our 1970 cohort of patients and families has been quite different. In the period immediately following release from the index hospitalization, the great majority of the recent patients entered outpatient treatment. Male patients were more likely to plan treatment while still hospitalized (female patients more often denied that they needed any treatment) but more than three-fourths of both male and female patients received some form of psychotherapy (usually coupled with drug therapy) and all but one of the others continued drug therapy in the early weeks after their return home.

Among those hospitalized in the 1970s, both patient and spouse were predominantly positive about outpatient treatment during the early months, though roughly one-third discontinued treatment before the end of six months. During this early period the spouse was involved to some extent in therapy (e.g., attended some therapy sessions) in slightly more than a fourth of the families, although the spouses seldom reported gaining much from the experience. Roughly three patients in 10 were rehospitalized within six months, mostly for a brief period; all but one was back home at the six-month follow-up.

It is of interest to examine the ways in which patients and spouses report their coping strategies at times of significant upset by the patient. During the initial six months after the patient's release from the original hospitalization, major upsets were likely to result in intensified outpatient treatment or rehospitalization, but less severe upsets were handled either by joint efforts of patient and spouse to resolve tensions (often making situational adjustments) or by simply doing nothing and waiting for the upset to resolve itself. This was, of course, the orientation of many of the couples in the period antecedent to hospitalization. For wives, the ability of the husband to hold a job appears to have been a critical consideration in deciding whether to ride with periods of upset or to seek a separation. Many of the marriages were terminated when husbands reentered the hospital, especially in the instance of schizophrenic patients whose level of functioning was considerably less effective than that of men with affective diagnoses.

Later Treatment and Help-Seeking

For the original cohort, follow-up interviews with the spouse or other informant were carried out, on the average, from 15–20 years after the patient's initial admission to a mental hospital. As of the time of follow-up, four of the 44 women and seven of the 36 men in the original sample had died. Seven of the women could not be traced into the recent past but it was possible to secure at least minimal data on all the men. The great majority of those for whom data were secured were in the community at the time of follow-up (97% of the men and 91% of the women). Roughly 90% of the women had received some form of formal psychiatric treatment—usually both inpatient and outpatient treatment—in the years intervening since they were first hospitalized. By contrast, 60% of the men had received treatment during the same period.

Perhaps the first question to be addressed is whether the greater use of treatment services by the women represented more severe and persistent mental disorder or a greater tendency to use mental health services. The answer would appear to be that both conditions prevailed. The majority of patients of both sexes had been diagnosed schizophrenic, but since we studied only married patients, our male patients tended to have a much more favorable prognosis. Only about a third of those males who are at sometime diagnosed as schizophrenic marry; those who do tend to have been more socially competent prior to onset and appear much less likely to become chronic patients (Zigler and Phillips, 1962). Marriage does not connote any such favorable prognosis for women. This general tendency found in many studies receives further support from the greater duration of early symptoms on the part of the female patients and the greater prevalence of hallucinations and bizarre delusions.

More direct evidence is available for that subsample of men and women for whom we have interview data on symptoms and family coping behavior in recent years. Of the women who were reported to have experienced persistent serious symptoms subsequent to initial hospitalization, all had some subsequent treatment; of nine men comparably symptomatic, however, three have had no treatment except for brief periods immediately following the index hospitalization.

When treatment experience is examined in five-year periods, the proportion of female patients readmitted to a hospital or remaining in hospital declines steadily from the first to the third period (table 1). More than three-fifths were rehospitalized within five years of their initial admission while less than a third were rehospitalized between 10 and 15 years after admission. Outpatient treatment, on the other hand, became somewhat more frequent; in the third five year period more than half of the women had outpatient therapy in a mental-health facility or with a private therapist. Men were also somewhat less likely to be rehospitalized in the third as compared to the first and second periods, but the decline was from roughly a third to about a fifth. Outpatient treatment of men increased more sharply than that of women in each five-year period but remained well below that of women.

TABLE 1

Percentage of Male and Female Patients Entering into or Remaining in Treatment, Inpatient and Outpatient, in Successive Five-Year Periods Subsequent to Release from Index Hospitalization

Hospitalization Period	Males		Females	
	Inpatient	Outpatient	Inpatient	Outpatient
First Five Years	31	6[a]	65	41[a]
Second Five Years	37	24	53	52
Third Five Years	21	31	32	62

[a]Excludes patients who had outpatient treatment as direct follow-up to index hospitalization.

Subsequent Hospitalization Decisions

We have noted that for the group of patients first hospitalized in the 1950s, women were more frequently committed than were men. In the period subsequent to that first hospitalization, however, the picture changed markedly. If we consider the most recent hospitalization of patients for whom we have reasonably complete data, 44% of the men but only 25% of the women were committed. Even when the men were not committed, their reentry into the hospital or their entry into outpatient treatment was less often the patient's decision and more often that of the spouse and/or of medical authorities. Female patients, on the other hand, who had most often been treated coercively at initial hospitalization, were far more likely to reenter treatment on the basis of their own decisions.

If husband and wife stayed together, as three-fifths of our original sample did, wives of male patients were twice as likely to play a major role in their husband's reentry into treatment as were husbands of women patients. It should be noted, however, that wives were far less likely to stay with symptom-ridden husbands; with only a few exceptions, persistent symptoms on the part of a husband led to separation and/or divorce.

There appear to be two reasons for the differential shift in type of admission over the years. Male patients seem, after a period of years, to evaluate their earlier hospital experience less positively and to be more concerned about the stigma of hospitalization than female patients. But a more important explanation of the differential derives from the greater tendency to rupture the marital bond in the face of continued symptoms by the male patient. As noted, relatively few wives were willing or able to tolerate the uncertainties of continued marriage to a man persistently impaired in his functioning, while husbands of seriously symptomatic female patients often managed to maintain their wives at home. Frequently the wives decided on separation at the time of a rehospitalization of the patient. Subsequently these patients went to live with parents, siblings, or other blood relatives. These relatives often found it difficult to deal with the patient in periods of upset. If they were unsuccessful in persuading the patient to seek help, they then turned to commitment procedures. Among readmitted patients in intact marriages, a fifth were self-initiated and two-fifths initiated by others but voluntary; among separated or divorced patients, 19 of 23 were committed on their most recent readmission to a hospital.

Recent Symptoms and Treatment—Less than half of the men for whom we have reasonably current data from interviews showed significant symptoms within five years of the follow-up. The most frequently reported symptoms for this group were nervousness, flare-ups, and depression. Hallucinations and delusions were relatively rare. Among female patients, however, four-fifths were reported to have had some significant upset within five years of follow-up and nearly two-fifths had experienced delusions and/or hallucinations.

The most recent expression of seriously symptomatic behavior might or might not be coterminous with the most recent entrance into treatment. Female patients in particular were likely to seek treatment, most often on an outpatient basis, when they were markedly upset. Nevertheless, less than half of these episodes resulted in treatment.

An intact marriage does not by any means insure that treatment will be sought for a distressed former patient. Roughly two-thirds of the marriages of male patients and half of those female patients seem to be reasonably good, and in these marriages spouses expressed considerable sympathy for the patient's distress. Nevertheless, the dominant response to such distress did not entail a high measure of active participation by the spouse in seeking to resolve the source of tension. Instead the dominant response was either nonhostile noninvolvement, or, where the marriage was less good, hostile detachment. This may help to explain why women, more often distressed and less often able to count on a sympathetic spouse, turn more frequently to formal treatment facilities than do men. Wives of male patients less often seem to be a direct source of the patient's upset behavior than do husbands of female patients. Moreover, wives more frequently indicate that they have seen the upset coming because of "signs" of one sort or another. Husbands of former female patients indicate that they are in general not aware of their spouse's upset until it actually occurs. For example, one man reported that he is usually not aware of any problem until his wife tells him that she wants him to drive her to the state hospital.

In some instances, the spouse seems to be almost totally impervious to the patient's needs. In others, one feels that the spouse and the patient have worked out a mode of coping with upsets that can hardly be regarded as supportive and yet appears to permit both husband and wife to continue to function at some level. Thus, the wife of a man who was hospitalized with a diagnosis of schizophrenia 20 years prior to the follow-up reports that her husband has had no subsequent psychiatric treatment but has had occasional periods of deep depression. In general, they have a good close relationship, but she reports that when he is depressed and wants to be alone: "We don't talk about it. I think it's best just to let him work it out." She has feared that he might kill himself, but neither she nor her husband think of psychiatric treatment as a possible resource.

There is much evidence that when the symptoms presented do not precipitate crises, husbands and wives go back to the patterns of coping that characterized the prehospital period. That is, they are more inclined to wait and see than to seek help except in cases of real crisis. Episodes of manic behavior, for example, almost always elicit action to commit. But where the problems presented are less acute, it appears that women patients are more likely to step up the frequency of treatment and drug use and that male patients are more likely to use alcohol and to be abusive of their spouses.

Our data do not permit us to delineate with any precision the various types of responses toward the use of treatment facilities that are characteristic of different types of patients. Class differences in our sample are small and not significant. The lower social status of female patients means that they have less resources to draw upon, yet they are more likely to make use of outpatient facilities.

Relatively few patients of either sex have consulted private psychiatrists in any period since release from the index hospitalization. A number of patients are being sustained by general practitioners, but it was not possible for us to distinguish those who are being treated for psychiatric problems from those who have chronic physical problems—high blood pressure, hypoglycemia, etc. We do know that their physicians frequently prescribe minor tranquilizers and occassionally major tranquilizers. Some may receive a measure of emotional support as well. But so far as their spouses know, at least, consultation with the physician is not primarily for emotional upsets.

Attitudes Toward Drug Therapy—Roughly two-thirds of the sample of patients hospitalized in the 1950s had taken major tranquilizers, antidepressants, or lithium on a regular basis for some period of time following the index hospitalization, and more than half were currently taking some psychotherapeutic drug at least occasionally at the time of follow-up. Except for the several instances in which lithium appeared to have terminated a long series of manic-depressive episodes, attitudes toward the continued use of drugs were at best ambivalent. This was equally true in the new cohort of patients entering treatment in the 1970s, of whom all but one were advised to take some psychotherapeutic drug after release.

In the period immediately following hospitalization, the great majority of patients appear to have followed prescribed drug regimes, though often with qualms. Nearly a third of the patients complained about side effects, especially sedation, and spouses were even more bothered by witnessing such effects. A fifth of the patients feared drugs; their symptoms had greatly increased immediately following their ingesting or being injected with some prescribed drug, and they were convinced that the drug had precipitated their original psychotic episode. Others felt stigmatized or feared loss of autonomy.

In the months and years that followed, spouses of patients on regular drug regimes complained that their husbands or wives were lethargic and unresponsive as a result of medication. Continued use of drugs connoted dependency and weakness, especially for men (whether patient or spouse). Some spouses openly disparaged patients who relied heavily on pills to get through difficult situations, and a number of patients felt that their continued use of drugs stigmatized them. They were likely to cut down or eliminate such use.

On the other hand, a number of women who deplored their dependence on medication managed to secure drugs from multiple sources, sometimes storing them against future needs or taking drugs in amounts and combinations that far exceeded prescribed levels. In several instances where major tranquilers were being used, it appeared that no real monitoring was taking place; the patient simply made a monthly visit to pick up supplies. Occasionally it appeared that the prescribing psychiatrist or physician preferred to have as little to do with the patient as possible but was willing to continue supplying medication. Under conditions of such heavy use in the absence of severe symptoms, spouses expressed very negative attitudes both toward the effects of the medication and the prescribing physicians.

Discussion

The findings here reported reflect the experience of patients and spouses in two local areas which are probably above average in the availability of a wide range of mental-health services. The patients had all married prior to their first admission to a mental hospital and therefore had a somewhat more favorable prognosis than hospitalized mental patients in general. Nevertheless, the help-seeking efforts of these patients and families, and their experience with treatment facilities are probably not markedly different from those of families with unmarried patients, though the participation of unmarried patients in help-seeking may well be somewhat different.

Severe mental illness has diverse manifestations. By and large, the psychotic person who exhibits manic behavior or has delusions of persecution is not oriented toward seeking help from medical or psychiatric facilities. On the other hand, the person suffering from diffuse anxiety or depression, or one who fears his or her impulses to harm others, may seek help. Most often, however, it appears that the primary decision to turn to medical or psychiatric facilities for help must come from family members or others close to the problematic individual.

Our data support the finding of Horwitz (1977b) for a sample of somewhat less severely disturbed first-admission patients that self-labeling of a psychiatric problem is somewhat more frequent than self-referral. Spouses, associates, and professionals are a more frequent source of early referrals than is the distressed person, and for our more severely symptomatic group, they are also a more frequent source of labeling the problem a psychiatric disorder.

In general, the more disruptive and threatening the patient's behavior, the less likely it is to be initially viewed within an illness frame of reference by the spouse and other family members. But if disruptive and bizarre behavior impinges upon others outside the family, so that those others comment to the spouse about the problematic behavior, earlier medical and psychiatric consultations are likely to take place. The previously mentioned research of Horwitz (1978) found that persons with open friendship networks (multiple nonlinked friends) were likely to enter treatment with the least severe problems and in the shortest period of time because the problem was more likely to be recognized and labeled by someone with a knowledge of appropriate treatment sources.

The sexes appear to differ markedly in their responses to a disturbed spouse. Men were less likely to recognize the extent of turmoil experienced by their wives, less likely to be sympathetic, and more likely to commit their wives even when the wives had expressed their need for help. Yet men more often delayed seeking professional help for their wives despite long histories of grossly bizarre behavior. Although our data do not bear directly upon feelings of stigma, the response of husbands to their mentally ill wives seems in keeping with Farina's (1980) observation that males more often act in ways that impute a stigma to mental illness, despite the lack of a sex difference in expressed attitudes toward mental illness. This may also help to explain the greater reluctance of male patients to seek treatment subsequent to initial hospitalization, and their higher ratio of commitment to voluntary admissions over the intervening years. Women tend to return to treatment on their own; men do not. In general, our data suggest that males are more threatened by the acknowledgment that they need help for an emotional problem, but both men and women who have been hospitalized have difficulty in acknowledging that they were unable to control their own thoughts, feelings, and behavior.

There is another sex difference that deserves comment, one that appears related to marital-selection processes. We have been struck by the frequency of severe character disorders among the husbands of female patients, especially schizophrenics. Some of those husbands are stable, competent men, devoted to their wives, but a number have long histories of occupational instability and disorderly careers. More than a few are alcoholic and/or show poor impulse control and gross insensitivity in their dealings with others. The marriages of these couples were often spur of the moment affairs; neither husband nor wife was aware that the other had experienced problems of long standing before they married.

Men showing character disorders were seldom oriented toward the use of psychiatric services as a means of dealing with personal distress, whether their own or that of their wives. They were more likely to be hostile to (or occasionally assaultive of) their wives than emotionally supportive of them. By contrast, the women who married men later diagnosed as schizophrenic were far more controlled and competent, on the whole. Thus, some of the sex difference found in our research may be due to the different selection processes in the marriages of preschizophrenic men and women.

Attitudes toward treatment appear to vary both by proximity to the initial breakdown and by subsequent treatment experience. In the period immediately following initial hospitalization, both patient and spouse appear to be most favorably disposed toward psychiatry and the treatment process. Subsequently, however, especially if there are continued episodes of symptoms and impairment, much more negative feelings are expressed, especially by patients. A decrease in favorable attitudes toward hospital treatment beyond six months after return was similarly reported by Weinstein (1979) in his review of research on patient attitudes. In the most extreme instances, patients or family members report that they would avoid future contact with psychiatrists as long as they could do so. A few blame the treatment received prior to initial hospitalization for the patient's acute breakdown. More often it is the lack of any startling change in the patient that leads to a negative evaluation of psychiatric therapy. This is especially true in the case of severely neurotic patients and chronic schizophrenic patients as contrasted with patients receiving manic-depressive or other affective diagnoses.

Relatively few of the married patients whom we followed up have been totally immobilized by mental illness over the 15–20 years since their initial acute episode. A sizable proportion have repeatedly needed help but only a few have become "typical" chronic cases. Many—primarily women—have a tie with a clinic or mental center which provides them with psychotherapeutic drugs and occasional monitoring or even group therapy sessions. But, as noted, there is in general little enthusiasm expressed for the treatment received; the dominant orientation of the patients and spouses interviewed toward psychiatric facilities and services was negative. Perhaps this was to be expected, given the self-doubts that many patients must project upon those who seek to be helpful. On the other hand, the attitudes of patients and their families may be to a considerable degree an accurate reflection of the kind of care being provided. It appears that few psychiatrists invest themselves heavily in the care of chronic patients; many may assume that anyone requesting help who was previously hospitalized must therefore be a chronic patient. The not-infrequent supplying of drugs without adequate monitoring further attests to serious deficits in psychiatric outpatient services.

One facet of our findings that has particular relevance for epidemiologic research is not directly related to help-seeking. It pertains to the fact that nearly half of the married men in our sample who had been hospitalized with a diagnosis of schizophrenia (and who met the much more rigorous criteria for such a diagnosis in DSM-III) had no treatment, inpatient or outpatient, subsequent to that initial hospitalization. Had they not been hospitalized 15–20 years ago, they would not have shown up in statistics of schizophrenia. Some have functioned well with no serious symptoms in the intervening period. A few have been persistently symptomatic but managed to get along without treatment, somewhat impaired in their functioning but by no means disabled.

We know that in some instances, these and other patients had had previous episodes of markedly disturbed behavior which had been self-limiting and terminated without professional help. It is quite possible that there are in the general population significant numbers of persons who at some time or other have had a period of psychotic symptoms that might warrant the diagnosis of schizophrenia had they sought help. We doubt, however, that the number of persons who *recurrently* present psychotic symptoms without seeking help is at all substantial. Families can live with seriously symptomatic behavior for months and sometimes for years, but ultimately the disturbed behavior is likely to lead to crises that can only be resolved by turning outside for help.

Only a relatively small proportion of psychotic patients and their families look to psychiatric facilities primarily as places that will make patients feel better; for the patient's spouse, the social-control functions of psychiatric help are most often those sought in taking action. This is not to say that husbands and wives are totally insensitive to the anguish of a disturbed spouse. Where psychotic manifestations are bizarre and disruptive, however, the criteria that lead to action appear to have more to do with the maintenance of social order than with treatment as such.

Acknowledgments

This research was supported by Grant MH-19649 from the National Institute of Mental Health through the Institute of Human Development, University of California, and by additional funding from the Grant Foundation (1975–1978).

References

Angrist, S.S., Lefton, M., Dinitz, S., & Pasamanick, B. (1968), *Women after Treatment: A Study of Former Mental Patients and Their Normal Neighbors.* New York: Appleton-Century-Crofts.

Brown, G.W., Birley, J.L., & Wing, J.K. (1972), Influence of family life on the course of schizophrenic disorders: a replication. *Brit. J. Psychiat.*, 121:241–258.

Clausen, J. & Yarrow, M.R., eds. (1955), The impact of mental illness on the family. *J. Soc. Iss.*, 11:3–64 (entire issue).

Farina, A. (1980), Social attitudes and beliefs and their role in mental disorders. Read at Workshop on Research on Stigma, National Institute of Mental Health, Rockville, Maryland.

Freeman, H.E. & Simmons, O.G. (1963), *The Mental Patient Comes Home*. New York: Wiley.

Greenley, J.R. (1979), Family symptom tolerance and rehospitalization experiences of psychiatric patients. In: *Research in Community and Mental Health*, ed. R. Simmons. Greenwich, Conn.: JAI Press, pp. 357–386.

Horwitz, A. (1977a), The pathways into psychiatric treatment: some differences between men and women. *J. Hlth Soc. Behav.*, 18:169–178.

Horwitz, A. (1977b), Social networks and pathways to psychiatric treatment. *Soc. Forces*, 55:86–105.

Horwitz, A. (1978), Family, kin, and friend networks in psychiatric help-seeking. *Soc. Sci. Med.*, 12:297–304.

Mechanic, D. (1968), *Medical Sociology*. New York: Free Press.

Myers, J.B. & Bean, L. (1968), *A Decade Later: A Follow-up of Social Class and Mental Illness*. New York: Wiley.

Sampson, J., Messinger, S., & Towne, R. (1964), *Schizophrenic Women*. New York: Atherton.

Weinstein, R.M. (1979), Patient attitudes toward mental hospitalization: a critique of quantitative research. *J. Hlth Soc. Behav.*, 20:237–258.

Yarrow, M., Schwartz, C., Murphy, H., & Deasy, L. (1955), The psychological meaning of mental illness in the family. *J. Soc. Iss.*, 11:12–24.

Zigler, E. & Phillips, L. (1962), Social competence and the process-reactive distinction in psychopathology. *J. Abnorm. Soc. Psychol.*, 65:215–222.

Notes on Contributors

DAVID MECHANIC, editor of the third volume of our series, is Professor of Sociology and Social Work and Acting Dean of the Faculty of Arts and Sciences at Rutgers University in New Jersey. Formerly, he was John Bascom Professor of Sociology (1973–1979) and Director of the Center for Medical Sociology and Health Services Research (1972–1979) at the University of Wisconsin. His special areas of research interest and scholarly endeavor include medical sociology, evaluation research and social policy, social psychology, health-care organization, and deviant behavior. Current research includes studies of the organization of medical and psychiatric care, adaptation to stress, decision-making processes in medicine and psychiatry, illness behavior, and comparative medical organization. Dr. Mechanic was elected to the Institute of Medicine of the National Academy of Sciences in 1971 and again in 1976. He is currently or has been a member of the Panel on Health Services of the National Academy of Sciences (1969–1973), Chairman of the Panel on Problems, Scope, and Boundaries of the President's Commission on Mental Health (1969–1973), the Epidemiologic Studies Review Committee of NIMH (1968–1973) and the Council of the American Sociological Association (1977–1978). He has served on the editorial board of numerous journals including the *Journal of Health Policies, Policy and Law* (1975–), the *Journal of Health and Social Behavior* (1965–1969 and 1972–1975), and the *Journal of Medical Education.* In 1977, he won a John Simon Guggenheim Fellowship and was elected a Fellow of the American Association for the Advancement of Science. Dr. Mechanic has authored or coauthored 100 books and papers. Currently, his address is the Office of the Dean, Faculty of Arts and Sciences, 18 Bishop Place, New Brunswick, New Jersey.

GEORGE W. BROWN is Professor of Sociology at Bedford College of the University of London, Regent's Park, London, NW1 4NS, England.

JOHN A. CLAUSEN is Professor of Sociology and Research Sociologist at the Institute of Human Development at the University of California, 1203 Tolman Hall, Berkeley, California 94720.

SUSANNAH GINSBERG is a Research Officer in the Social Research Unit of the Department of Sociology of Bedford College,

University of London, 51 Harly Street, London, NW1 4NS, England.

CAROL L. HUFFINE is Lecturer in Sociology and Assistant Research Sociologist at the Institute of Human Development of the University of California, 1203 Tolman Hall, Berkeley, California 94720.

HOWARD LEVENTHAL is Professor of Psychology at the University of Wisconsin, 1202 West Johnson Street, Madison, Wisconsin 53706.

DAVID NERENZ is Project Associate in the Department of Psychology at the University of Wisconsin, 1202 West Johnson Street, Madison, Wisconsin 53706.

NANCY G. PFEFFER is Research Assistant at the Institute of Human Development at the University of California, 1203 Tolman Hall, Berkeley, California, 94720.

MICHAEL SHEPHERD is a Professor of Psychiatry at the Institute of Psychiatry of the University of London in DeCrespigny Park, London, SE5 8AF, England.

ANDREA STRAUS is a Research Assistant in the Department of Psychology at the University of Wisconsin, 1202 West Johnson Street, Madison, Wisconsin 53706.

BLAIR WHEATON is an Assistant Professor in the Department of Sociology at Yale University. His current address is 140 Prospect Street, New Haven, Connecticut 06520.

PAUL WILLIAMS works with Dr. Michael Shepherd at the Institute of Psychiatry of the University of London in DeCrespigny Park, London, SE 5 8AF, England.